Praise for

FREE US

"Winning our battl vorld
will take more tha. Yet
one group is curren faith. In this book,
Coughlin gives us pasoning and inspiration as well as a realistic game plan against bullying. It's a must-read for anyone who cares about our culture, especially our hurting children."

　　—Barbara Coloroso, international anti-bullying expert and author of
　　The Bully, the Bullied, and the Not-So-Innocent Bystander

"I know of no one who is more passionate or better equipped to help navigate the depths and complexities of peer-to-peer child abuse than Paul Coughlin. Both informative and inspiring, this book is not only a valuable resource for parents, pastors, and educators, but for everyone who knows that just being nice isn't enough if we truly want to protect kids."

　　—Pete Kelley, lead pastor at Antioch Church

"Paul Coughlin has been an inspirational hero in the fight against bullying. *Free Us from Bullying* is a must-read for anyone concerned with sparing our youth from the crushing loss of self-esteem caused by this behavior."

　　—Leigh Steinberg, CEO of Steinberg Sports and Entertainment

"Justice speaks to the very nature, character, and heart of God, but justice is missing in the lives of millions of bullied children throughout the world. *Free Us from Bullying* will change this. It is a clarion call for people of faith to combat bullying the way we have combatted other forms of oppression."

　　—Ken Wytsma, founder of The Justice Conference and author of
　　Pursuing Justice

"Paul Coughlin has authored a beautifully written book about the tragic impact of bullying, showing us how it keeps us from a flourishing life in God while outlining practical steps to move forward in grace. This is a much-needed book."

　　—Roy Goble, cofounder of PathLight International and author of
　　Junkyard Wisdom

"In this book, Paul Coughlin helps us understand the ever-changing landscape of bullying and uses relevant and meaningful interviews, examples, and Scriptures to reach proactive solutions. As a school superintendent, I am constantly working to reduce bullying in organizations and communities. Paul is an incredible advocate in this work."

—**Dr. Paul R. Gausman,** superintendent of Sioux City Community School District and participant in the award-winning film *Bully*

"Some leaders prefer to just talk about a problem rather than fight for a solution. Paul Coughlin, however, not only exposes the evil of bullying that torments our children but also illuminates a safe path that leads them to freedom. I am thankful Paul allows God to use his pen and voice to speak to a nation that is failing to protect our children."

—**Jason Wilson,** founder and director of the Cave of Adullam Transformational Training Academy

FREE US FROM BULLYING

To Chloe

From Grampa

With lots of Love

FREE US FROM BULLYING

REAL SOLUTIONS BEYOND BEING NICE

PAUL T. COUGHLIN

LEAFWOOD
P U B L I S H E R S
an imprint of Abilene Christian University Press

FREE US FROM BULLYING

Real Solutions beyond Being Nice

L E A F W O O D
P U B L I S H E R S
an imprint of Abilene Christian University Press

Copyright © 2018 by Paul T. Coughlin

ISBN 978-1-68426-020-1 | LCCN 2018023020

Printed in the United States of America

ALL RIGHTS RESERVED
No part of this publication may be reproduced, stored in a retrieval system, or transmitted in any form by any means—electronic, mechanical, photocopying, recording, or otherwise—without prior written consent.

Scripture quotations, unless otherwise noted, are from NET Bible®. Copyright © 1996–2006 by Biblical Studies Press, LLC. http://netbible.com. All rights reserved.

Scripture quotations marked NIV are from The Holy Bible, New International Version®, NIV®. Copyright © 1973, 1978, 1984, 2011 by Biblica, Inc.® Used with permission. All rights reserved worldwide.

Scripture quotations marked GNT are from the Good News Bible. Copyright © 1994 by the Bible Societies/HarperCollins Publishers, Ltd., UK. Copyright © 1966, 1971, 1976, 1992 by the American Bible Society. Used with permission.

Scripture quotations marked NASB are from the New American Standard Bible®. Copyright © 1960, 1962, 1963, 1968, 1971, 1972, 1973, 1975, 1977, 1995 by The Lockman Foundation. Used with permission.

Scripture quotations marked NEB are taken from the New English Bible. Copyright © Cambridge University Press and Oxford University Press 1961, 1970. All rights reserved.

Published in association with Books & Such Literary Management, 52 Mission Circle, Suite 122, PMB 170, Santa Rosa, CA 95409-5370.

LIBRARY OF CONGRESS CATALOGING-IN-PUBLICATION DATA
Names: Coughlin, Paul T., author.
Title: Free us from bullying : real solutions beyond being nice / Paul T. Coughlin.
Description: Abilene : Leafwood Publishers, 2018.
Identifiers: LCCN 2018023020 | ISBN 9781684260201 (pbk.)
Subjects: LCSH: Church work with children. | Bullying—Religious aspects—Christianity.
Classification: LCC BV639.C4 C675 2018 | DDC 302.34/3—dc23
LC record available at https://lccn.loc.gov/ 2018023020

Cover design by Bruce Gore | Gore Studio, Inc. | Interior text design by Sandy Armstrong, Strong Design

Leafwood Publishers is an imprint of Abilene Christian University Press
ACU Box 29138, Abilene, Texas 79699

1-877-816-4455 | www.leafwoodpublishers.com

18 19 20 21 22 23 / 7 6 5 4 3 2 1

To targets of bullying,
wounded and oppressed:
you are God's beloved.

Contents

CHAPTER ONE

The Real World of Bullying

WHEN ALEX MOORE, A FIFTEEN-YEAR-OLD SOPHOMORE FROM JEMISON, ALABAMA, APPROACHED THE CHILTON County Road 48 Overpass, I don't think she had tears in her doe-shaped eyes as she stared down at the asphalt highway. Nor do I think she hesitated before slipping off her dull brown clogs and stepping onto the squat, skull-white concrete barrier on that humid morning of May 12, 2010. The same holds true for her head-first leap into morning traffic.

The mild afternoon before this fateful day, Alex had sat in the passenger's seat of the family's car as her mother returned home from Jemison High School. "I could tell she was very upset," her mother Jill later told me, "that something really bad happened. But she wouldn't talk. She sat there, stone-faced. Then later that evening, an odd calm came over her. She was . . . peaceful." Then

Alex completed a kind of modern-day miracle. "She even did the dishes without being asked."

That night, Alex cleaned and organized her bedroom with blonde wood paneling, simple single bed, and small wooden desk. On her desk sat a framed picture of herself as a yellow belt. Her hands are over her head. She's balanced and powerful, and appears ready and even eager to pounce and defend herself. I know it sounds irreverent, but each time I look at it, I see Kung Fu Panda in a similar pose.

That photo makes me chuckle because it doesn't add up, making it comic. And it makes me indignant because it gives the illusion of strength, vitality, and hope, but a force as powerful as gravity neutralizes them all, making it tragic. And it makes me sad because it's so misleading as to be a lie, like the lies our culture tells millions like her each day. Alex was quiet and shy, never a fighter. She had power in the ways that all of us have power, hopes and dreams, but like so many targets of serial bullying, her power didn't actualize and thus didn't help deliver her from evil. Like so many adolescents today, she was lied to by our culture, causing her to think that all pushback and fighting is wrong. That somehow in defending herself she'd be "lowering herself to the bully's level," "be just as bad as them," and "be a bad Christian," the common and deadly platitudes we adults dole out like cheap Halloween candy to children each day, thinking we're making the world a better place.

Around 6:30 A.M. she rolled out of bed, but instead of putting on her school uniform of khaki pants and navy-blue shirt, she wore a sweatshirt and comfortable black pants. She pulled her straw blond hair back into a ponytail and put on the silver, double-heart necklace her mother gave her for Valentine's Day. Its inscription read, "A Mother Holds Her Daughter's Heart Forever."

After making her bed, as if she were returning, Alex quietly closed her bedroom door behind her and walked down a narrow hallway lined with family photos. She went outside where the air hung warm and moist.

A girl her age should be dreaming about her bright yet uncharted future, giving her butterflies. She should be thinking about the boys who would cross her path, giving her even more butterflies. About weekends with family and friends. The screenplay she was finishing. About her desire to serve her country through the Air Force after graduation. College. Her eventual Prince Charming. Instead, Alex had mortality on her mind.

She turned eastward and marched through the ribbons of dawn's light onto the shoulder of Chilton County Road 48 in Clanton, a rural town of nearly nine thousand residents. Had Alex turned right instead of left, within less than a mile she would have walked by the home of one of her many tormentors, Brandon McFarland, whom she had gone to school with since first grade.

Brandon, unlike many of his classmates, didn't start bullying Alex until ninth grade, when he and others called her a fat $#&* almost every school day on the bus, in hallways, in gym class, in the lunchroom—wherever authority was absent, negligent, or both.

He joined his fellow tormentors during PE class, Alex's Ground Zero of humiliation, isolation, and rejection. There, Alex hid as best she could in the corner with her back against the wall, literally and figuratively. During her self-sequester, she read books about how best to nurture and heal animals while being pelted on purpose with whatever kind of ball was available.

She hid to get off her classmate's predatory radar, those classmates who through their body language, facial expressions, and words reveal a truth so disturbing that we as a nation fail to believe it: bullying is pleasurable. It's delicious. It's a mountaintop experience as you stalk, trap, and corner your prey. To control, dominate, and destroy another human being fills us with sinister glee. As the Good Book says, there is pleasure in sin for a season.

Brandon and his partners in crime savored Alex's psychological fragmentation, which is part of the definition of sadism. Yet most everyone would consider Brandon and his classmates "normal" and "decent kids." Studies show that most adolescents are attracted to bullying, not averse to it. The reasons are many, as we'll see later.

That morning, Alex must have appeared to neighbors as just another schoolgirl going for a morning stroll. If only a neighbor had sensed her grief and seen that something was plainly wrong with this overweight girl with Blount's disease, which caused her lower legs to bow outward. Her condition made it difficult and painful for Alex to exercise, so she was not known for morning walks.

She approached the final concrete driveway on her right, just yards from the overpass. Morning traffic sounds like ocean waves from there. Then she walked the final 0.4 miles along that shoulder-less, forgettable country road.

Just before 7 A.M. she jumped headfirst into southbound traffic. She plummeted for approximately 1.2 seconds and traveled nearly twenty-six mph before impact. The driver of an 18-wheeler saw Alex's body comet to earth and was barely able to halt his massive rig in time. "I was at her side in about thirty seconds," he told Alex's mother as he cried. "She was dead when I got to her."

When the space shuttle *Challenger* exploded just seventy-three seconds into flight off the coast of Cape Canaveral, Florida, on January 28, 1986, killing all seven aboard, President Ronald Reagan attempted to console an inconsolable nation. He quoted a portion of a poem by pilot John Gillespie Magee Jr. called "High Flight." It's about the ecstasy of escaping gravity, discovery, and the unique form of freedom that only flight provides. Reagan quoted its most memorable line of how those who fly dare to slip "the surly bonds of earth" to "touch the face of God."

That morning, Alex Moore shuttled downward not to escape the surly bonds of earth, but the evil bonds of arrogance, ignorance, and sadism, the wicked trinity of bullying. I believe she plummeted like a still-born meteor given the previous death of her spirit, to touch the face of God, then fall into his lap exhausted, broken, and with the hope that he would somehow drain the caustic water dammed within her soul. Poisonous water put there by other children, some of whom went to church.

I once believed young women like Alex cried before their deaths, the way they do in movies. But that was before I understood their desperate desire for relief. I have had hundreds of school-aged children wrap their arms around my neck after I speak in their schools about our disjointed war against adolescent bullying. They come from every background: physically challenged, mentally challenged, smart, dull, privileged, poor, straight, gay, and every shade of flesh. They convulse in my arms as if possessed. That's because they are. Part of their body, spirit, and soul is owned by their classmates.

Freeing Us from Bullying

Upwards of 70 percent of targets, like Alex, don't tell anyone. One reason is that many targets lack even basic words to convey their inner terror, in part because adults have not prepared them for the real world of bullying. A more saddening reason for their silence is because they don't believe adults will create meaningful solutions. Their reticence has merit since many adults cannot provide a working definition of bullying, nor real solutions to free these children from their misery.

Their path toward freedom is obstructed by wishful thinking and many damaging misconceptions (which are explored in Chapter One), such as how children who bully come from broken homes.

Another obstacle to overcome is how many adults perceive the leading form of child abuse in America to be a "school problem." In reality, parents, not teachers, are the frontline defense. We must change how we parent and what we value as a people if we are serious about protecting our children, curtailing mental illness and adolescent suicide, and reducing school violence, including shootings, all of which are associated with bullying. We need to reframe this issue and see that bullying is a cultural problem (the subject of Chapter Two).

The impediments to freedom from bullying are many, and some are formidable, such as the burden of the Niceness Doctrine along with its Magna Carta, the Golden Rule. This well-meaning but hazardous doctrine (the subject of Chapter Three) goes like this: *when I'm nice to you, you are obligated to be nice to me.* It's an especially attractive belief to church people, yet it can be deadly in the wrong application, like serial bullying. Bullies eat through the Niceness Doctrine like termites through punky wood. Instead, they respond to power greater than their own. And to consequences. That's their two-part love language, and we need to speak it to them sooner rather than later. This book helps us speak their language for the betterment of all children, including the serial bullies—because the sooner we can really reach them, the sooner we can arrest their budding criminality and help turn their lives around. No child is disposable, including the serial bully.

Bullying represents the worst in human nature—such as arrogance, contempt, and disdain—but combatting it brings out the best in us as well—such as kindness, compassion, and especially courage, the virtue that supports all other virtues. As explained in Chapter Four, children who stand against bullying without becoming bullies themselves, what this book calls "resistance without war," become stronger, more righteous, more courageous, and successful adults. If we truly want strong children, we must help them stand against bullying, which can also provide an avenue to profound spiritual growth.

Americans currently believe that the only viable response to bullying is the nice and gentle response. A primary reason for this mistaken belief comes from badly skewed pop psychology with its unwarranted affirmation and its pseudo-religion of self-esteem, which dogmatically claims that children who bully are really beautiful-but-injured doves of potential peace and love who are battered at home or broken in other ways that are hard to discern. "Whatever we do," I've heard too many mothers say to me during community events across this country, "we should never bully the bully!"

Their hearts seems to bleed for these "misunderstood" children who just can't seem to "control their anger" and so lash out at others "to feel better about themselves" because they suffer gravely from "low self-esteem." It's a script that is more familiar to us than the preamble to our Constitution or the Beatitudes. Yet as seen in Chapter Five, it is also blatantly false. This characterization of children who bully has been dismantled by facts dating as far back to the early 1970s by a leading pioneer in the anti-bullying movement, Dan Olweus. But we don't want to believe that people, and children in particular, do bad things simply because they find them enjoyable.

The hard truth is that the vast majority of serial bullies do not have lower self-esteem than their peers. Instead, many have inordinate self-esteem, the foundation of narcissism. "It is self-love, not self-hate," that compels schoolyard bullies, writes Roy Baumeister, who was initially an early evangelist for the Self-Esteem Movement in America, but who defected because the facts didn't add up. Baumeister is far from alone in his findings, as we'll see later in Chapters Six.

The forest of bullying is egregious, besetting, and terrible. But there is a way through this bramble of misconception, treachery, hatred, and related sins detailed in the beginning of this book. As explained in Chapter Seven, God hates bullying, so he is with us and will bless us as we defend the dignity of all children, regardless of distinction. Through partnering with the Association of Christian Schools International (ACSI), as well as working with entire public school districts across the country, I know what works to bring love, light, and hope into the theater of bullying. Part of the answer, as seen in Chapter Seven, is helping targets appear less attractive to bullies, most of whom aren't looking for a fight but to overwhelm. Among other proven strategies, this chapter helps targets appear more confident, even when they don't feel confident inside.

Though God hates bullying, too many Christians don't. One reason, as seen in Chapter Eight, is the misuse of Scriptures that unintentionally enable bullying. Chief among these Scriptures is a tortured interpretation of "turn to them the other cheek" (Matt. 5:39 NIV). As this chapter explains, this and related verses have nothing to do with a child being bullied in a bathroom, locker room, bus, or any other bullying hotspot.

Chapter Nine is an epicenter of change, doing what a ten-year landmark study by the Department of Health and Human Services revealed: to stop bullying, we must transform passive witnesses into courageous protectors, those who deploy decisive, positive peer pressure to denounce bullying. Our organization, The Protectors, has inspired students to do so for more than a decade, in part by appealing to what Lincoln called our "higher angels" and bolstering their capacity for courage, among other behaviors outlined in this chapter.

Creating an army of Protectors—these blessed peacemakers who are called "children of God"—is essential for another reason. Many targets do not have it in them to push their bully back. It's a leading reason why they are targeted in the first place. Like women ensnared by human trafficking, targets of serial bullying like Alex Moore require outside intervention and rescue. I believe that if Alex had just two Protectors, possibly even one, she might still be alive today.

And finally, this book ends by enlisting another group of people we will need if we are going to win our unofficial, and currently disjointed, battle against bullying. And as seen in Chapter Ten, we adults, people of goodwill, must commit ourselves to creating greater acts of Shalom and justice through what a remarkable 2003 study called "Authoritative Communities," which blends the wisdom of the sciences with the blessings of connection to one another and the Divine, what the authors call "hard-wired to connect."[1]

When surveyed, both parents and students place bullying at the top of their list of concerns. It's a national problem and worry, exacerbated by social media and our increasingly contentious and coarsening society. Its seriousness is underscored by the growing number of teen suicides linked directly to bullying, and how revenge against bullying is the primary motive behind most school shootings, revealing how although bullying isn't always evil, sometimes it is.

This book may turn your preconceptions about the causes and prevention of bullying upside down. I hope so, because what we're currently doing isn't working.

Because it's a fundamental component to our flawed human nature, and because it's so pleasurable, we will never fully eradicate bullying. But we can, and will, substantially reduce it.

To do so, we will have to get over our illicit love affair with niceness, which I hear about at every Parent Night presentation. "Aren't we supposed to love these bullies?" I'm asked. "We just can't throw bullies away!" I hear. Of course not. For reasons explained later, we're throwing them away right now through our nice approach, which fails to confront on a soul level. What we're currently doing isn't love—it's acquiescing. We're explaining away and even rewarding bad behavior from little monsters who grow up to become big monsters.

There is nothing unchristian or unkind about getting tough on bullying, nor about rearing children who are both kind and tough, compassionate and courageous—depending on what they need, what others need, and what God requires of us all. I believe it is unchristian to rear children to believe that they are required to accept intentional, repeated, and often increasing forms of abuse toward themselves and others. That they must remain the playthings of others who enjoy their pain and suffering and who mock their tears and cries for help. I remember those days all too well as a child.

Instead of hearing naive and mistaken Bible-flavored messages that sometimes express more compassion for bullies than for targets, what Alex Moore and millions like her really need is instruction about the necessity of verbal self-defense and assertive body language, the incredible value of being made in the very image of God, and other pearls of wisdom that greatly reduce bullying. She needed shrewd advice similar to what Emily Flake dispensed in two *New Yorker* cartoons.

One reveals with devastating clarity just how naive adults are when it comes to advice for targets. It illustrates a boy who has just been punched in the face by a bully and who is laying on the ground, humiliated and hurt. His nice and naive mother lectures him through one of the most popular and misguided messages within popular culture today: "Now Marcus, I want you to stop concentrating on Noah's (the bully) actions and focus on what's in his heart." What's in the average bully's heart isn't pain but pleasure, disdain and contempt toward others. Do we feel better now?

In the other cartoon, and at the other end of the parenting spectrum, she draws a concerned and shrewd father who says to his young child just before he enters a playground, "Son, if you can't say something nice, say something clever but devastating." Emily Flake was "eminently bullyable" as a child. "I had no real social skills to speak of, I was chubby, I wore glasses, my last name is Flake, et cetera," she told me. "Kids have an exquisite nose for blood, and I was chum in the water. The eighties, man, they were the worst! I wish that I had been given some tools or advice that would have helped me see a way to fight back." Millions of other children feel and think the same way. This book is for them.

Clever, devastating, shrewd, and *penetrating* are words rarely associated with Christian behavior, but are behaviors Jesus Christ himself commended through the Parable of the Shrewd Manager (Luke 16) and employed himself through such seemingly unchristian proclamations as these: "How much longer must I be with you and endure you?" (Luke 9:41); "Let the dead bury their own dead" (Luke 9:60); "Blessed is anyone who takes no offense at me" (Matt. 11:6); "[To Peter] Get behind me, Satan"(Matt. 16:23); "Depart from me, you accursed, into the eternal fire that has been prepared for the devil and his angels!" (Matt. 25:41); "Do not think that I have come to bring peace to the earth. I have not come to bring peace but a sword" (Matt. 10:34); "Do not give what is holy to dogs [referring to certain people]" (Matt. 7:6); "Concentrate your attention on the bare essentials, so you'll live, really live, and not complacently just get by on good behavior" (Luke 16:9 *The Message*); "The one who eats my flesh and drinks my blood has eternal life" (John 6:54); "The one who has no sword must sell his cloak and buy one" (Luke 22:36); and we're told that those who followed behind him were afraid (Mark 10:32) among many, many other examples. By today's standards within much of church culture that values niceness over goodness, kindness over more mature expressions of love, and hardly puts spiritual courage on our spiritual radars, Jesus was a very bad Christian. Given his clever, devastating, shrewd, and penetrating behavior and words, he might not even be "saved."

He did not suffer fools or bullies like the Pharisees, and neither should our beloved children. It's well past time to stop playing nice and start combating the only form of abuse we tell the most vulnerable among us to "just ignore."

NOTE

[1] Kathleen Alexia Kovner Kline, "Hardwired to Connect: The New Scientific Case for Authoritative Communities," Center for Global Integrated Education, Fall 2003, accessed on May 20, 2018, http://www.cgie.org/blog/resources /papers-publications/project-summary-hardwired-connect-new-scientific-case -authoritative-communities/.

Piercing the Darkness of Bullying, with Frank Peretti

Best-selling author Frank Peretti wrote *Wounded Spirit*, part memoir and part manifesto about his personal struggle with being the target of serial bullying during his school years. I had the opportunity to interview the sixty-six-year-old writer who popularized Christian fiction. His interview reminded me that if there's intensity, there's a story. Frank expressed palpable sorrow and anger when we retraced his experiences with being the target of ongoing abuse and cruelty at school. Even at his age, and with so much success under his belt as an author, he reminds us how we don't just forget the terror and humiliation from the punches, kicks, spit, and verbal assaults of our bullies.

Q: Tell us a little about your experience with bullying.
Bullying carries with it an almost right-of-passage idea. It just isn't dealt with. Not until recent days have people thought it was wrong and that we should do something about it. I was told to

"Just ignore it." "It happens to everyone." "Be a man." As a kid, you're locked into a situation you can't fix. You go to school, to a Scouts meeting, and so on. I didn't feel there was anything I could do about it. As far as I knew, I just had to take it.

I came from a Christian home that believed in nonviolence, where I was told to "Turn the other cheek," and where if someone abused me, I was supposed to take it. I remember specifically in grade school, this boy shoved me to the ground. I sprang up and got face-to-face with him. But there was this barrier I wasn't allowed to cross. I wasn't allowed to defend myself, so I just glared at him. From then on, he knew he had an easy target because he knew I wouldn't resist him. He bullied me for years, and it was a direct result of the teaching that I got at home.

The fruit from not pushing back became devastating to me. It actually worsened the problem and opened the floodgates to more bullying, which followed me. Once you get the reputation as a target, it's like a cosmic vibe where from grade to grade, you're the one. Word gets around. The turn-the-other-cheek poster reinforces it. When you aren't allowed or don't know how to protect yourself, it projects. Like wearing a sign. It shows in your timid personality. It enhances bullying and feeds the problem.

Can you get a bully to stop by appealing to his or her humanity? I'm skeptical about that. Bullying is animalistic—part of our base nature. It's sin of course, and has a spiritual dimension that's vicious, dark, and violates God's creation. I tend to hold the position now that fighting back isn't such a bad idea—some form of push back.

Q: How did bullying affect you, then and now?
The bullying I experienced didn't make me a stronger person. It made me a wretch. Bullying made me socially timid during my early adult years. I was afraid I would say the wrong thing, do the

wrong thing, and make small blunders. All this scared me to death. I suffered a real lack of resilience. I knew I was being overly sensitive. Yet even when I recognized it, I couldn't do anything about it. I'd say to myself, "Don't be so sensitive." It didn't help.

In gym class, I was maligned and abused. That's just the way it was. It didn't occur to me that I didn't have to put up with it. My gym teacher was an "ultimate male," cruel and mean, and the boys picked up on it and wanted to be like him.

I don't know what physical education is like now, but back then, PE was for jocks to show off and for nerds to be humiliated. Some kids just don't belong in PE. They can't compete. They're the studious types—poets, philosophers, artists—and they don't belong. Gym class was a system and a breeding ground for deep humiliation because it involved life's greatest intimacies: body parts, pubic hair, and nakedness—things that can cause the grossest humiliation.

This fear and pain followed me into adulthood. I can think of one powerful example. During the Vietnam War, we were all concerned about the draft, though thankfully I had a high draft number. I don't know what in the world I would have done if I were drafted. Maybe kill myself because I couldn't go back into that alpha-male, abusive environment like what I experienced at school. It would all be there again, in concentrated form.

I can think of another example: it was when I signed up to go to school at Seattle Pacific. I was in the registry office and an upper-classman came in and immediately put me down for being a freshman. All those memories and feelings came back; that continuity never stops. It just keeps going from grade school to junior high to high school, and to registering for college. I walked out and stood on the street corner and said to myself, "I'm never going to college!" I could not go through all that again.

I became a kind of vagabond for a while. I became a musician, sort of. I played the five-string banjo in a bluegrass band and played in bars, which was an experience for a kid who grew up in a Christian home. Oddly enough, the banjo became something I shined at. It brought positive reinforcement, joy, and recognition.

All these early experiences threw a long shadow. I think bullying played a role in how I used to have a pretty bad temper, like when something would take the form of having power over me and against my will. Thankfully, I don't have as much trouble with anger now.

Bullying can make it hard to respect and trust authority and respond appropriately. I had a teacher who got his chuckles from being the top guy in class, putting students down. He had a terrible approach and would rub my nose in my mistakes. Education should be about building up young lives and helping them find their gifts and prevent the violation of their humanity.

Q: But Frank, things turned out very well for you. You're a success.

The Lord has us in his hands and has a plan for us. I learned to trust the Lord because he's so trustworthy. Once I was on an evangelical radio broadcast where I talked about bullying and told the host what I went through. He said, "But God used it for good, didn't he?"

I said, "Yes," but afterward I reflected on my answer. What I said was the right thing to say, what we're supposed to believe. If God used it for good, it's not in ways that I'm aware of. I can't say I'm a better person for being bullied. As I said earlier, it made me a wretch. What I would say now is, "You know, I can't think of one good thing that came of it!"

Q: You write that Christians need to "stand up" and "speak out" against bullying. What would you say to those who wonder whether it's appropriate for a Christian to stand up and speak out?

There is a heroic side to Christianity, to snatch others from harm and suffering. The Bible is full of heroics, something the evangelical church will have to embrace more. The namby-pamby side of Christianity won't cut it when it comes to bullying, including bullying from our culture. At some point, the church will have to rise up to this stuff or be buried by it.

Q: If you had a magic wand, how would you diminish bullying?
Communication is big. So get rid of the silence. Authority has to be willing to listen and do something about it. It's the entrapment, the sense of being trapped in this cauldron, that is so bad for children. I didn't talk to my parents because I didn't think it would do any good to tell them.

My parents made me participate in Boy Scouts, and there was a pecking order in our troop. The same thing all over again where "manhood" was defined by being macho—stronger and tougher than the little guy. I didn't like Scouts and didn't want to go. The Scout Master and I were avowed enemies.

Once my troop was on a campout and sleeping in the mud. The experience was miserable, and I started thinking, "Why do we build houses? Why do we build shelters for ourselves? Because we don't want to be out in the rain!" I mean, we even have an old saying: "Too stupid get out of the rain." We couldn't keep a fire going because of rain.

But the group kept talking about how this is what men do. This makes you a man. When I got home, I threw my stuff on floor and said, "If this is what it takes to be a man, I'm never going to be a man!"

Years later, a friend and I were sitting around the dinner table, and I shared this story from my scouting days. My friend looked at me and said, "Frank, you're a man with a capital M." It felt so good to hear that. The measure of a man is so much deeper than how macho a man appears.

Q: Many targets of serial bullying, when they do get help, get help from people who bend the rules, as was the case for you. Your counselor excused you from gym class by saying you had a condition. But you didn't have a condition. And it was this excuse that really changed your life for the better.
My counselor knew I was clearly being mentally and physically abused. He may not have followed the letter of the law, but he followed its spirit. He was concerned about me as a human being. As a counselor, he was supposed to go beyond and help the heart of students.

Q: What would you say to those who say, "Jesus suffered, so you should too"?
Jesus suffered for a particular reason. He was pierced for our transgressions; he was crushed for our iniquities (Isa. 53:5). He suffered for all this so we wouldn't have to. He became sin so we could become his righteousness. He bore suffering to defeat evil, which should not be misconstrued that we should let evil continue. His crucifixion established a new base for righteousness that compels us to battle against evil.

There is no point in repeating his suffering in terms of atonement. If you're going to speak to a little kid in school about Jesus, his suffering and the child's suffering, this is how you should put it, "Jesus suffered for our sins. What are you suffering for? He accomplished something through his suffering. You're not." We can't point out some large, cosmic good for the child's suffering at the hands of bullies.

There's no connection between the forms of suffering. We are giving kids poor theology and erroneous thinking.

CHAPTER TWO

Essential Insights into the Theater of Bullying

Courage is fire, and bullying is smoke.
—Benjamin Disraeli

THERE IS PROBABLY NOT A MORE MISUNDERSTOOD AND EXPLOITED WORD TODAY THAN *BULLYING*. SADLY, THE word is sometimes used to denounce whatever we don't like personally and has been weaponized to demonize those we dislike politically. It has even snuck its way into the world of sports as well. In the fall of 2013, after being trounced 91–0 in high school football, an unnamed father from the losing team, Western Hills High School in Texas, filed a formal complaint of bullying against the opposing coach, Tim Buchanan of Aledo High School (a team known for blowouts). As I wrote for Fox News, "Please, let's remove the word 'bullying' from all sports pages," because teams don't bully; individuals do. The perversion of this important word should cause us deep trouble since schools across the country are wasting precious time and energy on false claims of bullying that should be invested in real cases of child-on-child aggression.[1]

Bullying Defined

Adolescent bullying is not about conflict, misunderstanding, mis-communication, "drama," or related misconceptions. It is the deployment of repeated, superior power against another child, deliberately intending to harm that child for no justifiable reason. It is victimization without provocation. This power can take many forms, such as physical, social, and economic. But most of the time, it is verbal and designed to harm a child socially through humiliation, isolation, and threat of further abuse. Some definitions include audacity on behalf of the bully, which we at The Protectors include as well, because, as the old adage says, evil carries within itself the seed of its own destruction. For reasons explained later, it's a bully's audacity that may be one of only a few avenues in which to reach them and hopefully transform them.

As mentioned earlier, most bullies aren't looking for a fight. Most long to overwhelm another child. So they profile and cull from the herd certain children who they are pretty sure will accept their abuse. They target nice kids, shy children, and others who aren't assertive or don't appear confident. And this happens quickly. One reason why October is Anti-Bullying Month in America is because most bullies have selected their target by the end of September.

A Closer Look at Two Categories

Barbara Coloroso, in her outstanding work, *The Bully, the Bullied, and the Bystander*, lists seven kinds of bullies: the confident bully, the social bully, the armored bully, the hyperactive bully, the bullied bully, the bunch of bullies, and the gang of bullies. No one has created a better work than she when it comes to explaining this portion of the theater of bullying. But for our purposes, we will address two types of bullies that Coloroso addresses as well: acute and serial.[2]

Acute bullies experiment with bullying, the way youth experiments with drugs, alcohol, and sexual behavior. But this doesn't mean they become drug and sex addicts. The behavior doesn't define who they are. Many children find themselves playing the roles of bully, bullied, and bystander throughout their school years. I played all three roles as well.

Serial bullies are another matter. They are the ones who cause the most harm to others, and they usually don't stop. They are far more likely to commit some felony as young adults and abuse their future spouses and children. Nice appeals to the Golden Rule, but peace, love, and understanding rarely, if ever, change their behavior. To put their behavior into a more biblical framework, they are the kind of children and young adults who invent new ways of doing evil to others (Rom. 1:30). They are also the mockers described in Proverbs 3:34, those who sneer at and mimic others, treat them with ridicule and contempt, and who over-estimate their own abilities and intelligence. Yet most surprising to some, bullies are also highly self-righteous and are smugly intolerant of the behavior of others. This pride-swelling attribute gives their attacks a substantive self-justification that is difficult to remove. They sit in judgment of their classmates, often deeming them as inferior. And most, contrary to myth and misconception, love the role. While decent people view the bully as the villain and antagonist, she sees herself as the protagonist. That's because, due to inordinate self-love, not self-hate, she sees herself as one meant to rule. What's wrong with the world isn't her—it's her target.

Most bullies cherish their role since it is electrifying to control others. It's pleasurable to dominate others, and it feeds our ego to believe we are superior to others. These traits and more reveal what we don't want to see: serial bullies share a similar mindset with criminals, rapists, racists, and more.

Courage and *Thumos*

Studies show that most children know and feel that bullying is wrong when they witness it (about 80 percent). But they don't act upon what they know and feel. When it's within their power to act and they don't, in most cases it is due to a lack of courage—or to put it another way, the sin of cowardice (Rev. 21:8). This is why we focus on courage creation throughout this book. And just as we say emotions are found in our hearts and understanding found in our minds, the Greeks told us that courage is found in our *thumos*, our chest and lungs. Our thumos is where our thoughts and feelings wrestle and are turned into courageous action or not. Lack of courage, not a desire for kindness, empathy, and compassion, is what stops most bystanders from becoming Protectors. They want to help, but are too afraid.

The Problem with Kindness, Awareness, or Empathy Alone

Our world needs more kindness, awareness, and empathy. The problem is, by themselves, kindness, awareness, and empathy don't have the horsepower to create change. They must be energized by a functioning capacity for courage in order to combat bullying. This is one reason why courage is called the foundational virtue—because without it, we can't be kind consistently. And for reasons explained later, empathy can sometimes lead to unintended bias and even cruelty, and compassion is more effective for diminishing bullying than empathy.

Portal Moment

A portal moment is a time of change in our lives either for good or for bad. Bullying is such a moment since there is hardly any neutrality in the theater of bullying. Most every child is affected by it, including bystanders. For example, when bystanders witness bullying and fail to help the target when it's within their power to act, their capacity for courage, compassion, and kindness decreases in the future. This makes them "smaller-souled" people, and our word for that is *pusillanimous,* from which we have derived more than one derogatory word.

Contrast this to those who help targets. Their capacity for courage, compassion, and kindness increases in the future. They become larger-souled, or magnanimous, righteous and mature in love. Handling such portal moments righteously leads to great faith, courage, character, and leadership skills.

Hope before Love

In the life of a beleaguered person such as the target of bullying, hope is more essential than love, because if that person doesn't have a reason to believe in a better future, love won't have soil in which to grow. This is one reason why this book gives targets multiple plans of action, because if we supply targets with just one solution and it doesn't work (such as "Look the bully in the eye and tell them to stop"), hope may be lost.

Justice before Forgiveness

The word *justice* appears in the Bible about 130 times, compared to the word *forgiveness*, which appears about 13 times. God's Word emphasizes justice 10 times more than forgiveness, and yet many in church emphasize forgiveness much more than justice. As people of faith, we should be concerned about both.

Poor in Spirit

Targets of serial bullying belong to that beloved group of people that God says are blessed, and for whom he has a special love: the poor in spirit (Matt. 5:3). And when the Spirit of God came upon Jesus, he said he was anointed to proclaim good news to the poor (Luke 4:18). But to more than the poor. God sent him to "proclaim freedom for the prisoners and recovery of sight for the blind, to set the oppressed free (Luke 4:18 NIV). Targets of bullying are oppressed just as those in human trafficking are oppressed. They are different forms of oppression.

Doesn't Make Us "Stronger"

Wealthy and famous celebrities sometimes say that bullies made them the successful people they are today. And during Parent Night, I also hear adults say, "That which doesn't kill us makes us stronger." They think they're quoting the Bible, but they aren't. That's Friedrich Nietzsche, who hated the Bible and Christianity, and who also said, "Man is the cruelest of all animals." One study by the Wesley Society of Australia found that seven out of ten targets of serial bullies had great difficulty forming lasting adult relationships, trusting others, and had anger management problems. They especially struggled with resentment, a leading negative emotion tethering them to drug and alcohol abuse.[3]

One of those damaged targets was Alex Moore, whose bullycide (when the primary cause of suicide is bullying), says her mother Jill, was a desperate act of protest. Quiet and private Alex "wanted us to remember what happened to her, and then do something about it for other kids just like her." Jill believes Alex was miserable and a martyr, a young woman whose bodily death was but a belated death of her spirit. She felt that there was no way out for her, but perhaps she could create an exit for others.

Jill wanted answers after Alex's death. She discovered that the deliberate campaigns of cruelty against her daughter went on for years unabated. Classmates threw Alex's books off her desk and across the room. They mocked her and imprisoned her in closets and in bathrooms, sometimes for hours and with no light. They pulled her pants, *including her underwear,* down to her ankles in an attack that would bring lawsuits in the adult world, but in the theater of bullying, it brought glee and laughter instead.

"She was made fun of daily [by] heartless people, our peers, [who] teased her because she was not up to their standards," wrote a fellow student after Alex's suicide, who is still so traumatized by what she witnessed that she couldn't talk to me directly, and only communicated through email.

> Well, not a lot of people are. I wish someone would've told Alex that it's not what a lot of people say about you, it's about the few, close friends you have. I now value life itself and the people who love me, along with myself, much more. There's a lot of things people regret right now, and they should. But instead of focusing on what was said to her, I want to let you know what she shared with me. I talked to Alex every day at school. The day before this unfortunate event, she told me that she was tired of everything. She couldn't handle it anymore. "I heard that when you go to heaven, it's like your own idea of heaven," she told me. I like to think Alex is in a place right now with those who loved her, where she doesn't have to put up with the constant teasing she once had. I like to think that Alex is somewhere where she isn't hurting anymore.

Alex was the object of what the senior boys at Jemison called the "Pig Race"—they created a list of the girls they deemed to be the ugliest in school. Alex was atop this list of human trash. At the appointed time, the boys would run to just one, and kiss her on the cheek. Whoever got to the "pig" first won in a game that some would characterize as good, clean fun.

A neighbor alerted Jill and her husband Jim to what Alex's classmates wrote about her on Facebook while she was still alive. There they found textbook cyberbullying: words intended to sear her psychological flesh for the unforgivable sin of being overweight. In an amazing gesture of kindness, Jill contacted three of the cyberbullies, who all self-identified as Christians in their profiles, and asked if there was anything they wanted to tell her. Only Brandon McFarland responded. He asked for forgiveness, which Jill granted. More so, Jill commended him for his honesty and courage.

I spoke with Brandon.

Q: Brandon, you apologized to Alex about two weeks before her death. Why then?

I started going to Victory Baptist where I got saved. I began to realize the horrible things I was doing and to see the importance of other people more. I saw smaller details—you know, how people responded to things. The first giveaway was Alex's eyes. In the morning, they were bright and glistening. They had hope. But by gym class, they were old and droopy. She wasn't happy; she was hurting. The first place I started was with Alex. I walked up to her at the end of gym class [Brandon clears his throat, as he did many times throughout the interview] and asked her to forgive me. I couldn't look in her eyes I was so ashamed of myself. She looked at me for about five to six seconds then went back to reading her book. It was the last time I talked to her.

Q: What happened when you found out about Alex's death?

A lot of people were sad, and I was angry, mostly at myself. What I did helped her do it. It's something that eats at me every single day of my life. Something I did forced somebody else to make the worst decision of their life. I forced someone to kill themselves because of how I treated them.

Q: But you apologized, right?

I have an analogy: You throw a plate on the ground, and it breaks. You tell the plate you're sorry. Does that fix the plate?

Do you want to know what angered me the most the day Alex died? Most of the people who said they were friends with her were the same people who bullied her. One kid even said out loud during gym class, the same place where the worst bullying took place, "She deserved to die!"

Q: What did the other students do?

Most just hung their heads in shame.

How will Alex's bullies and bystanders exorcise the budding tumors of guilt and shame within their consciences? To whom will they turn in that town of many steeples, where children lift their hands and voices in praise to Jesus of Nazareth on Sunday, and then destroy one another on Monday? And where is our indignation that says, "Enough!"? Today is a good day to be angry because as Augustine understood, "Hope has two beautiful daughters: Anger and Courage. Anger that things are the way they are. Courage to make them the way they ought to be."

Notes

[1] This book corrects prevalent myths and misconceptions about the leading form of child abuse in the nation and probably the world, including many Christian and related religious beliefs that actually make bullying worse. It is not intended to be a definitive work about all aspects of adolescent bullying. For such works and related resources, please see the recommended reading list.

[2] Barbara Coloroso, *The Bully, the Bullied, and the Bystander: From Preschool to High School—How Parents and Teachers Can Help Break the Cycle of Violence* (New York: Collins Living, 2003).

[3] Jude Lobo, "Wesley Society of Australia Study," *The Wesley Report* 6 (2009), accessed April 9, 2018, https://www.wesleymission.org.au/news-and-publications/publications-and-resources/the-wesley-report/give-kids-a-chance-no-one-deserves-to-be-left-out/.

The Anatomy of a Serial Bully

I've been observing a serial bully the way a biologist would observe an animal in the wild. Of the roughly five different kinds of bullies, he falls squarely into the loudmouth and brutish camp. He isn't clever like the most dangerous kind of bully, but like the most dangerous kind, he is sometimes charming in order to get what he wants. He kisses up, and kicks down. If he were a cinematic character, he'd be John Fitzgerald, Tom Hardy's character in *Revenant*, full of grunts, simmering anger, schemes, mockery, and disdain toward others. Like Fitzgerald, he has a premeditated insult waiting on his lips, and he scans for opportunities to spit one out. Like Gollum in *The Lord of the Rings*, I have watched his physical features grow ugly and contorted. I've seen his face slide down as if it were liquid glass and form a near permanent schoolboy scowl and glare.

This towering bully is a veteran gossipmonger who constantly fishes for information about others. But not just any information. He only fishes for information that embarrasses or humiliates. He discards details that do not help him build a negative narrative about others. Virtuous behavior, such as generosity, has no utility in his bullying laboratory. And he doesn't care if the intel he seeks is true. It just needs to appear true.

He regularly bears false witness against others.

I'm embarrassed to say that I did not recognize his bullying ways earlier. A heads-up would have been helpful, but at that time, I was surrounded by the kind of churchgoers who believed that any negative information or warning about another person of low character was somehow gossip and "idle talk." If that is true, then much of the book of Proverbs is laced with gossip.

Making matters worse was a deadly strain of church teaching that encouraged me to accept any form of abuse because it came from the hand of God to improve my character. I was told that a bully could only be given a kind response because God would use my loving actions to transform his hard heart, making him a better person. For more than twenty years, this never happened. Instead, my kindness was continually used against me, allowing him to unleash more insults and embarrassments.

We train others how to treat us, and with the help of my naive spiritual training, I trained him horribly. I employed the usual excuses that other naive people used as well: *He's just in a bad mood. His life is hard. He doesn't really mean it.* None of this was true, since I watched him bully one moment then turn on the charm the next, depending on who was in front of him and what he wanted. Still, I denied what I really saw and heard. My church training told me I had no other recourse but to take it. Back then, I didn't know that another and more life-giving and biblical script existed. The simplistic and reductionistic script I was given gave me no cover, and he knew it. I was like a soldier in the middle of a field with not even a molehill for protection. He pinned me down.

That was many moons ago. I finally woke up by discarding that fraudulent script and obtaining a more comprehensive and biblical understanding of wickedness, and a wiser Christian response to it. I continued to observe and test him. I kept this covert, because once people know they're being watched, they clean up their act and put on a makeshift halo, even if it's crooked. I wanted to observe his unvarnished self. Here's what I observed:

- He defends fellow bullies, especially famous ones, and gaslights those who criticize famous bullies.
- He enjoys television shows where people are brutalized, embarrassed, and humiliated.
- He is unable to keep relationships going because eventually people just slip away from him without declaring it. They just don't call or come around anymore.
- He exposed within me a real struggle as to how to retain my own dignity and at the same time not respond out of anger and revenge.
- He speaks and acts as if he's still in high school.
- He is a living, breathing example of why Jesus told us not to give to dogs what is holy, nor cast pearls before swine.
- He revealed to me the mental and emotional chaos such people create in our lives, and the social grace they exploit as long as their exploitation is tolerated by those too easily led.
- Bullies can dish it out, but they cannot take it.
- He's encircled by enablers who cover up, defend, and deflect his behavior. Confront him and you will have to confront them as well. There's a better way: resistance without war (more on this later).

- He doesn't bully people who push back. He goes after the younger, timid, nice, and kind until they grow up and push back. Once they push back, they are no longer "good" people.
- He scorns the unintimidated.
- Kindness and compliments never spurred him to become a better person—not once.
- He doesn't compliment others and doesn't joke about himself.
- When in conversation, he doesn't listen to you. He's looking and listening *at you*, waiting like a boxer to verbally jab and punch.
- He has just enough religion to make him feel self-satisfied and impenetrable.
- He cherishes looking down his nose on minorities.
- He is far more interested in managing his public image than actually changing his soul. He reminds me of the maxim that the surface of a lake may change due to the color of the clouds above; but the lake remains the same.
- Like other narcissists, he craves attention, and pouts, scowls, mocks, and snickers when someone else gets it.

I see now that my attempts to humor him just made matters worse. Funny isn't it? We're against rewarding bad behavior in children, but for some reason we're okay with rewarding bad behavior when it comes to adults. This is because we don't fear children the way we fear adults who bully—a testament to *our* cowardice.

Like Frank Peretti, I cannot say my experience with this person made me a better person. Many times, his slander and abuse caused me and my family great consternation and sleepless nights. What I can say for sure is that contending with him has opened my eyes to human wickedness, and how easily the simple are led. I gained greater wisdom, painful as it was, to the true character of a certain kind of person who makes up 5–15 percent of our friends, coworkers, family members, neighbors, and churchgoers. Today, I'm better able to defend children from wickedness and evil, and for that I'm grateful.

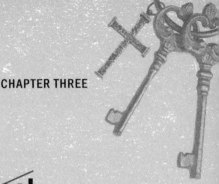

CHAPTER THREE

Bullying—Our ~~School~~ Cultural Problem

We are the inheritors of a coarsened society. My generation cooperated happily in the coarsening, of course, in the sixties and seventies . . . and now we're stuck with it. The coarsened nation is what we have left with to bring up our children. A coarse place is by definition anti-child because it is anti-innocence. —Peggy Noonan

THE TRAGEDY OF ALEX MOORE BURDENS OUR HEARTS AND HAUNTS OUR MINDS—NOT JUST FOR OUR OWN CHILDREN, but other children as well. Netflix's popular *13 Reasons Why,* based upon the 2007 novel by Jay Asher, has given our worry deeper contrasts and ominous colors. This controversial show revolves around personable Hannah Baker, who as a junior in high school commits suicide due to a series of personal and public calamities, most revolving around bullying.

Hannah leaves behind cassette tapes that contain explicit details about how she was mistreated and abused, and how humiliated, isolated, and alone she felt afterward. They show how cruel, callow, and ignorant youth can be in a culture that mistakes power

45

for strength and popularity for purpose. Critics took aim at it for glorifying suicide and over-stating the problem of bullying.

> After the premiere of "13 Reasons Why," the search phrase "how to commit suicide" rose 26% above what would normally have been expected for that time; "suicide prevention" went up 23%; and "suicide hotline number" climbed 21% based on the paper's data.
>
> "The time for rhetorical debate is over," said John Ayers, research professor at San Diego State University and lead author of the paper.
>
> "While '13 Reasons Why' has certainly caused the conversation to begin—it's raised awareness, and we do see a variety of suicide-related searches increasing—our worst fears were confirmed," he said. "That is, thousands of people, thousands more, are searching online about ways to kill themselves."[1]

While watching the series, I was at moments disquieted by the possibility of glorified suicide, especially one scene where Hannah looks behind her to see if a school administrator is going to chase her down and offer further help and emotional support. He doesn't, mostly due to the incessant ringing of his phone. As I wrote for *Fox News*, that scene could, in the mind of the immature, give the dangerous impression that agency over a person's life is a corporate, not personal, matter, that multiple hands are on the tiller of life when deciding to live or die.

I wish that scene had been treated differently. I also wish that endearing Hannah hadn't provided so many public displays of pain and anguish. I wish this not because I think Hannah shouldn't have felt so wounded and angry. (I know too well such feelings.) I wish she hadn't shown her feelings to her tormenters and had instead journaled, used meditative prayer, or talked to someone she trusted, because I know what public displays of pain and anguish do to a high schooler's persona and image. Such displays crush them socially, earning them the derogatory titles of "Drama Queen," "Momma's Boy," and worse names, even in Christian schools. They marginalize our children and open them up to more frequent and intense bullying in a culture that values homogeny and comfort more than fairness, appeasing bullies more than standing for what's right.

But something powerful and helpful got lost among our collective worry about this teen drama: bullying. Some complained that the creators over-dramatized high school life, repeating the self-soothing and heartless claim that it's not that bad. Or they're the kind of people who say, even during their middle years, they didn't have bullying in their high schools, when studies have revealed that this is nearly impossible.

Hannah Baker and *13 Reasons Why* worry us because we witness how even an intelligent, beautiful, funny, deft, but especially strong young woman can be taken down by serial bullying. She and Alex Moore provoke us because they could be our children. And if we've paid even slight attention to the news, we know they aren't alone. And these cases of bullycide that have appeared in the news are just the ones that made the headlines. Having worked with parents whose children took their lives due in whole or part to bullying, I know there are many more cases where grieving parents successfully prevented the news of their child's bullycide from getting into their local paper.

This series could have led to a deeper discussion about the true dynamics of bullying, but that opportunity has passed us—which is unfortunate because part of this deeper discussion would have revealed how what we value as a nation plays a role in the lives, and deaths, of our children. When we adults value lock-step conformity over real or perceived differences, our children witness it and do the same at school. We applaud and consume what we approve, so when our children witness us receiving pleasure and glee from reality television shows where people have their psychological skin seared from them, they think that expressing disdain and contempt toward others is fun as well. They bring these values into their schools. It's not the other way around. Schools do not lobby Congress in order to get funding to create Public Service Announcements that make expressing disdain and contempt toward others fun and exciting. Kids get their ideas and customs from us adults, making bullying a cultural problem, not a school problem. And studies confirm this.

One of the most comprehensive studies comes from researchers at UCLA.[2] They surveyed 1,895 ethnically diverse students from 99 classes at 11 Los Angeles middle schools and asked the students to identify the most popular students and then the bullies. The lists were nearly identical. Let's ponder this for a moment. The kids who bullied were almost always the most popular and admired in school. Most students in middle school look up to, not down on, peers who bully.

This UCLA study reveals how most students, like a growing number of adults, fail to distinguish between power and strength. Power (physical, verbal, economic, or social) is raw and feral. It spews, is selfish, and is unrestrained by common, or what used to be common, moral, or ethical codes of conduct. Because power is so delicious to wield, and because it brings to the wielder so many spoils of war, it's intoxicating. Worse, you don't just get what you want. You get it with style and swagger. You become a celebrity at school. You gain the rarefied glow and grandeur of dark celebrity, gaining the world but bartering parts of your soul, or as John Updike put it, "Celebrity is a mask that eats into the face." Power makes you and others believe you are above the herd, meant to rule.

Moral strength is filtered power, removing its self-serving elements. Strength retains influence and animating force, but without domination and control. It presides and radiates, drawing others toward the person without coercion. Strength encourages. It provides a degree of comfort to others but also urges them forward. It's not always nice and kind, because sometimes strong people create discomfort and even pain for the other's good. And strength, unlike power, carries with it maturing qualities of grace where all people are accepted and honored. But today, most adults could not point out this difference, so why should we expect our children to do so?

This comprehensive study reveals that being unkind, mean, cruel, and even wicked helps a child gain and maintain popularity. Where did our children get this belief and immoral currency?

The Explosion of Real Examples

We could identify many culprits, such as the growth of moral relativism, the objectification of people through pornography, video games, and other types of media or entertainment, the mudslinging and insults that characterize much of today's politics, the incessant negative campaigning that accompanies the election cycles—and the list goes on. But I would like to focus on a fairly new phenomenon within the world of television that encourages bullying and has taken popular culture by storm for more than thirty years: reality TV.

Before exploring this particular culprit of social harm, it's important to remind ourselves what bullying is really about. The anger we see on television isn't bullying in and of itself. Two political commentators passionately disagreeing and arguing isn't bullying either. Two people fighting over the same object of their affection isn't by itself bullying. Bullying involves degradation, the stripping of dignity, value, and worth through the belief that others are below you. Bullying begins with three deadly words, "I am special."

In order to degrade, we must first steal the dignity of another. Unless you're a psychopath or sociopath, you will need to find a "reason" in order to bypass or at least placate your conscience when contemplating and executing such thievery. Our culture, especially through the portal of reality television, has shown us the way. We see this often in shows where contestants battle for an ultimate prize, usually a pile of cash. But order to get it, they often appeal to "survival of the fittest," meaning they are more fit (physically as well as intellectually) than others. Therefore the other person deserves trickery, lying, and treachery. It's how the world goes round. On camera, they shrug as if to say, "That's how the game of life is played." Chumps with strong moral codes are weak, but people like them are strong. They don't just possess greater skills than others. They are designed to rule over others.

It has always been pleasurable to dominate, control, and manipulate others—well before reality television came on the scene. But what has changed is the social landscape in which this new medium grows and festers. The usual social mores and indignation against such behavior, such as feeling ashamed for treating others this way, have been dangerously weakened. And in some cases, they've been removed altogether. It's far cooler to be cruel than it was just twenty years ago.

Some of these shows have been redemptive, such as *Biggest Loser, Extreme Home Makeover, Undercover Boss,* and related programs that take bad situations and make them better, uplifting the contestants and their audience. They, of course, aren't the problem, and I hope we see more of this kind of programming because our culture, and especially our children, needs to see it. It's the other kind, the more popular kind, that's the problem.

Brave atheist Salman Rushdie believes reality television's success tells us much more about ourselves than the subject of the lens, and it's not pretty. "What tawdry narcissism is here revealed!" he writes, noting, "Who needs talent, when the unashamed self-dismay of the talentless is constantly on offer?" Then, his critique goes from a simmer to a boil:

> "Famous" and "rich" are now the two most important concepts in western society, and ethical questions are simply obliterated by the potency of their appeal. In order to be famous and rich, it's OK—it's actually "good"—to be devious. It's "good" to be exhibitionistic. It's "good" to be bad. . . .
>
> Add the contestants' exhibitionism to the viewers' voyeurism and you get a picture of a society sickly in thrall to what Saul Bellow called "event glamour." Such is the glamour of these banal but brilliantly spotlit events that anything resembling a real value—modesty, decency, intelligence, humour, selflessness; you can write your own list—is rendered redundant. In this inverted ethical universe, worse is better. The show presents "reality" as a prize fight, and suggests that in life, as on TV, anything goes, and the more deliciously contemptible it is, the more we'll like it.[3]

Rushdie believes we're being gradually reinvented into "gladiatorial combat," where our screen is the Coliseum and the "contestants are both gladiators and lions; their job is to eat one another until only one remains alive. But how long, in our jaded culture, before 'real' lions, actual dangers, are introduced to these various forms of fantasy island, to feed our hunger for more action, more pain, more vicarious thrills?"[4]

It's painfully easy to backfill examples into Rushdie's sweeping claims. I could spend the remainder of this chapter and possibly this book listing examples just from the life and times of celebrity chef Gordon Ramsey. His performances on *Hell's Kitchen* have earned him tens of millions in part by searing not just meat but the psychological flesh of others, all to the amusement of an international audience. His expletive laden tirades contain all the marks of a serial bully: sharp words, juvenile insults, and even fake striking—lurching like one would strike with a hand but recoiling at the last moment. Such behavior is a form of assault or harassment, depending on the state statute.

But who's making him wealthy? Adults, primarily. Adults tune in to watch him psychologically attack others. Adults are his bystanders who advertisers seem gleeful to have view their commercials, keeping Ramsey's bully train screaming down the rails.

When asked about his verbal abuse in an interview, he said it doesn't bother him, but it does bother his mum. And like Ramsey, many within our culture also dismiss his abuse in a tongue-in-cheek manner. "What makes this sort of bullying even more off-putting?" asks Ishaan Tharoor for *Time*. "That he's probably playing it up for the camera." So, is it worse when it comes from a less genuine place? The excuses we hand bullies.[5]

Far Too Accepting of Bullies

There have always been malicious people who act catty, snipe, gossip, back bite, start rumors, feed rumors, mock, slander, falsely accuse, and more. But we used to denounce these behaviors because, although we couldn't put it into words, we knew where such language could lead: spirit murder. Now our culture makes those who shame into wealthy celebrities. We need to get our character back. We as a people should be ashamed that we have made

Ramsay and others like him filthy rich, find his abuse funny, and label it as entertainment.

"We live in a culture," writes David Brooks, "that teaches us to promote and advertise ourselves and to master the skills required for success, but that gives little encouragement to humility, sympathy, and honest self-confrontation, which are necessary for building character."[6] How can a school, any school, combat such growing coarseness and failing character on its own?

Schools reflect the character of their community—rarely the other way around. Students bring this character into schools each day like dirt upon their shoes. In the case of South Hadley High School in Massachusetts, the tragic cite of the bullycide of Phoebe Prince in January 2010, the residents took on Ramsey-like qualities. E. J. Fleming marvels at the "inflated self-worth [that] flows like a river through the town and washes over the parents and children."[7] Facing such a tide of entitlement, there was little that the school could do to combat bullying in any meaningful way. In fact, Fleming reports that the parenting in that town was so negligent that more than two hundred parents of players in a football league received letters in 2010 demanding that they cease arriving drunk to games and stop drinking during games.[8]

The drum majors of self-debasement, such as Springer, Povich, and a host of imitators, clean up well. Under the pretense of being helpful, many television sensationalists and reality TV personalities bait delicious traps for others to reveal their most base behaviors to the entertainment of a live and virtual audience. They stage cliché fistfights between sexual partners, spurned lovers, and secret rompers. They manufacture obligatory who's-the-real-father announcements, as if a real baby's life isn't on the line, a pawn in the game of rank ratings. Yet many program their televisions to record each episode. And viewers and the studio audience give their applause. Then later, at school, students mimic this "reality behavior," cheering on and encouraging bullies and their free-for-all behavior.

Children Watch You Too

Children, our own and others, are watching us. They laugh at what we laugh at and applaud what we applaud. They find glee and entertainment in what we find glee and entertainment. They are our biographers who through the umbilical cord of modeling become what we become and approve what we approve. We adults have no stones to throw at today's adolescent bystanders because we're bystanders as well, sitting in the comfort, glow, and boredom of our own reality TV colosseum, cheering on the bad guys, becoming second-rate people ourselves.

Thug parents create thug kids who consume thug media, which studies have shown increases abusive behavior. It's a free world, so there's little people of goodwill can do to halt this consumption. But such thuggery is still a minority. We still have time to push back within our communities. We still have power in numbers. We must cultivate our indignation and denounce what we see and hear.

People of goodwill, it is time to transform our culture—first, through the refusal to consume media that encourages bullying behavior. Once we make that choice, we have hope that our schools will be transformed as well.

Let's take the Reality TV Pledge and vow to do the following:

1. We will only watch redemptive reality television where participants and the audience are built up instead of torn down.
2. If we do watch the other kind of reality TV, we will point out to our children that what is happening is wrong, and it's not funny. We will ask questions such as, "How would

you honestly feel if someone treated you that way? Your best friend? Mom or Dad? Your brother or sister?

3. Tell advertisers that you will no longer buy their products as long as they advertise on that program.

Notes

[1] Jacqueline Howard, "'13 Reasons Why' Tied to Rise in Suicide Searches Online," *CNN*, July 31, 2017, http://www.cnn.com/2017/07/31/health/13-reasons-why-suicide-study/index.html.

[2] Jaana Juvonen, Yueyan Wang, and Guadalupe Espinoza, "Physical Aggression, Spreading of Rumors, and Social Prominence in Early Adolescence: Reciprocal Effects Supporting Gender Similarities?" *Journal of Youth and Adolescence* 42 (2013): 1801–10, https://doi.org/10.1007/s10964-012-9894-0/.

[3] Salman Rushdie, "Reality TV: A Dearth of Talent and the Death of Morality," *The Guardian*, June 9, 2001, https://www.theguardian.com/books/2001/jun/09/salmanrushdie.

[4] Rushdie, "Reality TV."

[5] Ishaan Tharoor, "Workplace Users and Abusers: Gordon Ramsay," *Time*, October 18, 2010, http://content.time.com/time/specials/packages/article/0,28804,2025898_2025900_2026132,00.html.

[6] David Brooks, *The Road to Character* (New York: Random House, 2015), iBooks.

[7] E. J. Fleming, *Tread Softly: Bullying and the Death of Phoebe Prince* (n.p.: Hall Hill Press, 2012), Kindle.

[8] Fleming, *Tread Softly*, Kindle.

Do Our Lives Matter?

My people, targets of bullying, eventually wonder if their lives really matter. They don't believe that other lives don't matter. They know all lives matter. It's their own that they question.

They question their own value, dignity, and worth because of what bullies do and say. And because of the silence of bystanders.

We are incurably social beings who need one another to affirm our value. For someone to confirm that the injustice we experience is really unjust. When we don't get this confirmation, we begin to go mad, get mad, or both.

Targets and their families tell me that institutions and individuals let them down. It's rarely intentional, but still they feel like they are on the outside looking in. However, it's the way bystanders remain silent in the face of their persecution that makes the victims of bullying shake their heads even more.

Here's how I help them, and how we can drain the pain of others who question if their lives matter. It's not political. It's human. I listen to my people and confirm their pain. I tell them that I'm sorry, that they aren't crazy, and that I'm here to help.

Affirming a beleaguered person's pain makes their pain less toxic. It's an act of grace and love. In most cases, they aren't asking you to make things right for them. They're asking, without asking, for a kind of soulful amen. *I'm sorry that happened to you. It was wrong.*

Racism, bullying, and bigotry are links in a formidable chain that is forged by harmful pride and galvanized by a hunger to feel and appear superior to others. It's a tempting hunger most of us have felt at one time or another; but most of us don't give in to it. Racists, bullies, and bigots do.

All lives matter, but there are those among us who have been led and pushed to believe that they are children of a lesser god. And they often get this heretical belief more through the silence of bystanders than from the perpetrators of disdain and contempt.

CHAPTER FOUR

Nice and *Dead* Can Be Four-Letter Words

Being nice to my bullies just made things worse for me. One told me she didn't want my prayers and told me to kill myself. —Jennifer Martin, Christian educator

WHEN DR. STANLEY MILGRAM, THE SOCIAL PSYCHOLO-GIST WHO SHOCKED THE WORLD DURING THE 1960S WITH his obedience to authority experiment, wanted to underscore the power of his devastating findings regarding humanity's shocking ease in harming one another, even to the point of murder, he provided a detailed description of his experiment to different groups. Sometimes, he pulled in Yale seniors, a group of psychiatrists, or even middle-class adults.

In his experiment, which has been repeated and confirmed many times since, an unknowing subject was told to administer electrical shocks to another person when that person failed to provide the right answer to a series of questions. Even when the setting on the fake electric shock machine read, "Danger: Severe Shock XXX," and even when the naive subject behind the fake lethal switch heard cries of agony and pleas to stop the experiment (the actor playing the role of the one being shocked would even tell the unsuspecting subject before the testing began that he had a heart condition), Milgram found that 65 percent of the subjects pushed the button with a drone-like and "robotic impassivity" to obey authority, in this case an emotionless director sitting behind him in a white and sometimes gray lab coat. "We did not need Milgram to tell us that we have a deeply ingrained propensity to obey authority," writes Thomas Blass. "What his findings revealed is the surprising strength of this tendency—strong enough to override a moral principle we have been taught since childhood—that it is wrong to hurt another person against his will."[1]

When Milgram asked members in these groups how many people they thought would obey orders to shock another person to the point of probable murder, their answers were so wildly wrong that they might cause a person to question the wisdom and understanding of anyone who claims to be an expert. Yale seniors, supposedly among the most educated in the nation, said that only 1.2 percent of people would provide the strongest shock, revealing a potent and naive prejudice toward the innate goodness of humanity. A group of psychiatric residents at Yale were dismal in their prediction as well. In a letter to social psychologist E. P. Hollander, Milgram complained, "The psychiatrists—although they expressed great certainty in the accuracy of their predictions—were wrong by a factor of 500."[2] For those like me who are horrible at math, that's 50,000 percent.

That poor prediction is from experts, or experts in the making—people who should know better because they possess, or claim to possess, special insight into the labyrinth of the human psyche.

Milgram put smelling salts under the world's nose that showed us just how pedestrian evil can be. Milgram showed us is that such common evil isn't an anomaly. Our world is packed to the rafters with people willing to blindly follow authority, even to the point of murdering another human being because he failed to provide the right answer to a series of inconsequential questions.

The "experts" were so wrong that it justifies lampooning. Instead, some went on the offensive. Psychologist Bruno Bettelheim claimed Milgram's research was "so vile that nothing these experiments show has any value. . . . They are in line with the human experiments of the Nazis." A Benedictine monk from Washington, DC, wrote to Milgram, unleashing his revulsion: that was an "extremely callous, deceitful way in which the experiment was conducted."[3]

I have also challenged deeply held presuppositions about human nature and felt the wrath of those who breed and protect the sacred cow of human goodness, people who refuse to acknowledge the depth of human depravity and dogmatically cling to a more comforting and pleasant view. They are evangelists of the Niceness Doctrine who perceive themselves as loving and moral, yet, as I hope to prove here, are reckless when offering solutions within the theater of bullying.

I've promoted a more muscular solution to bullying for more than a decade to many groups, but especially to the Christian church throughout North America, which is currently MIA. For all the church's truth, goodness, and beauty, it just doesn't believe it is needed in this battle to defend the weakest and most oppressed among us, right under our nose and no further away than the neighborhood playground. Yet we will travel overseas to combat other forms of injustice. Perhaps this is because like our prophets, we prefer, if not demand, evil and injustice at a distance, fearing somehow that we can't withstand the experience.

In reality, we can do far more than withstand the winds of injustice in our face or shoving us from behind. We can grow in righteousness and spiritual vigor. This book aims to diminish bullying and provoke such spiritual ripening because our current un-involvement is one of the main reasons why bullying is so prevalent and growing by the day. This world needs our light and salt and vision as a people on a holy mission: to bring God glory and benefit to man through spreading love, hope, and faith to all corners of the earth, including the neighborhood playground.

Nice or Good?

One reason why we as Christians are MIA is how we perceive our Christian rules of engagement when it comes to injustice and wickedness in general. We've been taught directly and indirectly that the only viable response to evil and the pain and suffering it delivers is niceness, an attribute never assigned to Jesus, his Father, or the Holy Spirit, and a word that doesn't even appear in the Bible, showing how the phrase "If you don't have anything nice to say, don't say anything at all" has no support from a biblical framework.

To promote any other approach is deemed by many, including some within today's trendy anti-bullying movement, as unbiblical and even dangerous. I have watched these inspirational speakers cycle in and now out of the theater of bullying. They added bullying to their cafeteria list of topics that public and private schools can choose from during student assemblies, and they provided the usual message of awareness and kindness.

They rode that wave, and are now onto the next hot topic: adolescent resiliency. These comely Christian inspirational speakers are big on zeal, but dangerously low on wisdom when it comes to bullying. Getting in on the action from one of the hottest topics throughout the last decade, they parrot our culture's wishful thinking when it comes to making the world a better place. And that wishful thinking revolves exclusively around today's pet virtues: the tender ones such as niceness, kindness, and compassion. It's what our world wants to hear, and they deliver. But it's the wrong

prescription to change the hearts and minds of the most dangerous culprits of the most perpetrated form of child abuse: serial
bullies. They cause the most damage by way of frequency and
intensity, and they are rarely swayed by such appeals, especially
as they grow older.

One such speaker, before a large audience of Christian educators, said that nearly all bullying ends when appeals to compassion
and kindness are gently gifted to those who bully—that is, when
he delivers the message. An administrator of a Christian school
for more than twenty years said afterward that if he followed this
speaker's pleasant prescription, he wouldn't have a school left to
run because the bullies would take over. In all his years of contending with serial bullies, he said he was never able to get one
to change his or her ways. His appeals to peace, love, and understanding, similar to the charismatic speaker we both just heard,
fell on deaf ears. A stronger approach, he said, is always required.

Another Christian inspirational speaker to students promotes
the Golden Rule of doing unto others what you would have them
do to you. He promotes this solution due to his deep acceptance
of the stated and unstated credos within evangelical culture, which
are at times a peculiar mixture of doctrinal and cultural preferences
and presuppositions, some of which have no viable connection to
the Golden Rule. His winsome message is also replete with heart-
felt pleas for fresh acts of kindness, niceness, and gentleness. He
adopted and promoted the now disproven belief that bullies are
misunderstood souls in need of the kind of love that will salve and
bandage their inner brokenness, transforming their inner caterpil-
lar into the big-hearted and splendid butterfly they were meant to
be. This is such a dangerous belief that it is also negligent.

I hear versions of the Niceness Doctrine during Parent Night
at public and private Christian schools where adults are adamant
that bullies should always be treated with kid gloves, forgetting

or perhaps never knowing that so-called compassion toward a bully, as well as her syncopates, is often cruelty to her target. These adults, usually women, mistake all expressions of force (an attribute of *virtus*, where we get today's word for *virtue*) as dangerous and immoral. Yet they would certainly abandon this belief if a burglar were to enter their home by calling the police and their lethal force. Such a person would likely contact the most powerful attorney in her city as well to protect her assets because that attorney is willing and able to use the full force of the law on her behalf. I'm amazed at how force-averse such people are—until they need force to create clear and healthy boundaries, which is exactly what targets need. Yet these people believe they are being nurturing, big-hearted, and "Christian." I contend that anything that doesn't lead to the flourishing of human life in its many expressions isn't Christian. This includes foolishness and naivety.

The Niceness Doctrine—a security blanket patched together through wishful thinking, Scriptures orphaned from the balancing benefit of the surrounding biblical truths, and pop psychology with roots deep into secular humanism—disintegrates when it becomes too expensive to keep on artificial life-support, when the petri dish it lives in is exposed to the real air, light, and weather of life. That place is school, including Christian schools, where studies show that weakness invites aggression from bullies, especially in middle school.

Contrary to earnest messages that radiate from within evangelical culture, including our credulous movies, is how serial bullies do not listen to wet-eyed pleas for peace, love, and understanding. They believe the Golden Rule is for suckers. Such people require stronger medicine, and that medicine is found in the same Bible that promotes kindness and gentleness when they lead to life, but then something more potent when they don't.

One of these misguided movies is *The Secrets of Jonathan Sperry*, starring Gavin MacLeod. Jonathan Sperry is a seventy-five-year-old spiritual grandfather to three twelve year olds who encourages them to live for the Lord. In response to a complaint about bullying from one of the twelve-year-olds, Sperry says, "If your enemy takes a piece of your pizza, offer him two." Within much of church culture, this is taken to mean that children should "turn the other cheek" and "go the extra mile" when dealing with bullies.

Turn to Him Your *Left* Cheek

There is probably no more popular Bible quote, nor more prevalent Bible confusion, in the theater of bullying than Jesus's admonishment to "turn the other cheek." This phrase is the foundational tenant of the Niceness Doctrine. Yet, as explained shortly, it's not even accurate. When kept in context with the two other examples that surround this phrase, we are better able to minister to the most hurting children among us.

> You have heard that it was said, "An eye for an eye, and a tooth for a tooth." But now I tell you: do not take revenge on someone who wrongs you. If anyone slaps you on the right cheek, let him slap your left cheek too. And if someone takes you to court to sue you for your shirt, let him have your [cloak] as well. And if one of the occupation troops forces you to carry his pack one mile, carry it two miles. When someone asks you for something, give it to him; when someone wants to borrow something, lend it to him. (Matt. 5:38–42 GNT)

Jesus, speaking to adults about adult situations, not children, and certainly not children who are being intentionally abused, used three illustrations with *legal* consequences:

1. A blow to the right cheek was a serious insult punishable by a heavy fine. This is likely why Jesus said to turn to the offender your *left* cheek since the right cheek had already been struck.
2. A person's cloak was protected from forfeiture (Exod. 22:25–27), presumably so the person would not be left naked and completely vulnerable.
3. A Roman soldier's right to commandeer civilian porters was limited to just one mile.[4]

The legal context to Jesus's three illustrations is fortified by the previous passage (Matt. 5:25–26), "Reach agreement quickly with your accuser while on the way to court, or he may hand you over to the judge, and the judge hand you over to the warden, and you will be thrown into prison. I tell you the truth, you will never get out of there until you have paid the last penny!" He's telling us that sometimes it's best to settle a matter out of court instead of asserting all of your legal right at all times. He may also be suggesting paying off a bribe so that you won't find yourself being extorted even more by crooked magistrates. Avoid legal entanglements, he's telling us, even if you are on the right side, because you may be saving yourself from unforeseen woes and sorrows.

Because of the context, it is possible, if not probable, that what Jesus is saying here when he said, "Do not set yourself against the man," is do not automatically go to court against a person who wrongs you. All three of Jesus's illustrations involve the possibility of setting aside legal rights *as an adult.* They have nothing to do with children being intentionally abused by another child or, for that matter, an adult.

It's as if Jesus is saying something like this: "You adults, we both know you have the right and freedom to sue that other person, to say 'no' when others burden you. To respond harshly when insulted. But should you? I want you to consider showing a generous spirit instead." I add *generous spirit* because look at how this section concludes: "When someone asks you for something, give it to him; when someone wants to borrow something, lend it to him." *This* is the main point Jesus is making, a point that isn't mentioned when addressing adolescent bullying from a Christian perspective. None of this falls in the category of physical, psychological, or spiritual abuse since these are single acts, not part of an ongoing pattern of abuse and sometimes terror.

If you have camped in a public campground, you may have been unfortunate enough to camp next to a person running his generator till 10 P.M., which is when the no-noise curfew kicks in. But up until that time, he will assert his right, and all the while make everyone else miserable. After all, one of the reasons you go camping is to get away from noise like that. But he does it anyway, garnering the frustration and anger of those around him as he asserts his rights. What Jesus is saying is don't be that guy who is right but also very wrong.

Taking into consideration *who* Jesus was talking to, *what* his main point is, and *how* he said it into the theater of adolescent bullying, here is a hypothetical statement that Jesus might say: *You and your family may have the legal right and freedom to sue the bully, but should you do so automatically? I want you to consider extending generosity to the bully and her family. This is what you might say, "You know what your child did was illegal. We could press charges, but we've decided not to in order to show you and your child generosity. We are also considering inviting you and your child to dinner, if that's something we can agree upon. But either way, we are also telling you that if your child harms our child again, we will take legal action. To be over-generous can be as harmful as being under-generous."*

When I mention this possible answer from Jesus to parents, the topic of forgiveness usually comes right up. Jesus's response to Peter is usually the first text mentioned. Peter asks Jesus how many times he is expected to forgive a fellow disciple. He proposes seven, and Jesus responds with "seventy-seven times" (Matt. 18:22), a number that symbolizes boundlessness. The context here is between disciples, not between a terrorized child and his terrorizing bully, an essential distinction.

The hypothetical statement provided earlier doesn't advocate unforgiveness. I'm advocating justice, fairness, and real compassion for targets. We can forgive another and at the same time erect strong boundaries, a truth made popular by Christian psychologist John Townsend. And forgiveness doesn't require reconciliation either. Sometimes allowing a bully back into the life of a target is the worst thing an adult can advocate.

Through turn the other cheek, Jesus, as usual, is redirecting our interior lives through admonitions to grow in expressions of love. And notice how in these three examples, there is no permanent damage done to a disciple, unlike bullying where affects can last a lifetime or even help end a life. He is not condemning the legal system of his time, and he is certainly not telling children or adults to allow themselves to be bullied to a pulp by allowing themselves to be continually slapped, punched, or kicked.

A generous spirit, in this case to go beyond what the law requires, doesn't advocate a foolish or ridiculous spirit. Logic states that if a person can be under-generous, then that same person can be over-generous as well, which is Jesus's point here. The fact that he addresses under-generosity instead of over-generosity is probably because we are far more prone to commit the former than the latter.

Jesus did not literally turn his cheek when struck by the guard of the high priest (John 18:23). He defended himself verbally and called the guard into account for his actions. What Jesus could also be telling us is that we shouldn't return an insult for an insult. We shouldn't partake in revenge. That isn't even close to what happened in *The Secrets of Jonathan Sperry*. A bully stole food from another person. (Studies show that most bullies already have what they stole from a target, showing that in this case the bully wasn't in need of food. Bullies steal not out of need, but to control, dominate, and humiliate others.) Imagine if we told adult Christians that if someone steals $100 from them, give him $200?! Most adults would object, and rightly so. But for some reason, when such horrible advice is given to children, we find it nice and adorable. Could it be that we don't really value children the way we should?

Our resistance within the church to a more muscular approach is real and sometimes unbending. One reason for this is because we don't really know how premeditated bullying can be. So let me give you one example. When children who bully hear that I'm coming to their school, they sometimes begin a misinformation campaign among students and even faculty weeks before I get there. Children as young as twelve. Remarkably, some of their parents will join them when talking with other adults, complaining that the school is "wasting their money again." These students will be among the first to say, "We don't have a bullying problem here." And, "What a waste of time." Children who bully and their followers will sometimes sit together at the side or back of the assembly and intentionally snicker, talk, and laugh while I speak to disrupt me because they know I'm a threat to their power base. (I know this because principals tell me afterward who they are.) They will tear down Protectors posters and work their dark magic in the classroom right after the presentation as well.

Recently, I spoke at a Christian high school in the South because two arrogant, entitled, and unrepentant bullies attacked another young man. The school was very fortunate they weren't hit with a lawsuit, and they knew it. So they wanted to make sure that they served God and their students well to make sure such an act of covert bullying wouldn't happen again. The bullies, with the blessing of their parents, skipped school the day of our presentation. One used it as an opportunity to check out another school. I can only imagine the conversations in their homes that week. I would bet that both the bullies and their families blamed the victim and played the role of the real victim, which is Bullying 101. Unfortunately, appeals to the Golden Rule, kindness, and niceness usually won't change such students or their families who are, regardless of church attendance, innately me-centered, not us-minded.

And at the same time, I have seen appeals to kindness and related virtues work with bullies, especially acute bullies and if the appeals are made before the entire school. I have helped compel thousands of children to apologize for bullying publicly before their peers, teachers, parents, and principals. I appeal to what Lincoln called their higher angels—but I also include more potent medicine, such as powerful comparisons between bullying and sexual crimes against women, racism, genocide, and how bullies are far more likely to commit felonies and abuse their future spouses and children after graduation. I explain that bullying is often just a fancy word for sadism, and I ask my audiences, "Is this what you want to be known for? Do you really want this to be part of your legacy?" I throw high heat at bullying because sometimes that's the only thing that gets their attention. Bullies have a what's-in-it-for-me mindset toward change, and so I give it to them.

I can't forget the senior at a Christian high school who, before 1,600 of his peers, was so melted by our message that he walked down from a flight of stairs in a California gym, took the microphone from my hand, and apologized to his target with his left hand gently slapping his heart in a touching display of contrition. He got a standing O. But he did so because I didn't coddle him, nor did I savage him. I told the truth in love, creating a safe place for him to repent, and he took it.

I have been fortunate enough to help thousands of students change their ways, in part by appealing to their inner sense of decency, kindness, and empathy. It's a sight to behold. Watching veteran teachers during these presentations is especially enjoyable to witness. They think they've seen it all. They haven't. They witness what they have always wanted to see, though never thought they would. Their tears are a testament to their gratefulness. Numerous teachers have told me afterward that our anti-bullying event in a public school felt like a "religious experience."

The ripple effect of these apologies is something no person can fully discern either. But we all know it is true, beautiful, and good—the three transcendental human ideals that correspond with science (truth), art (beauty), and religion (goodness). They will radiate throughout time and space and change personal histories within the larger arc of history, especially if the target is a sibling. But I also know something else. In the same audience where children find the courage and humility to apologize are hunkered down children who just plan to weather the storm I've brought. Instead of being hailed as a deliverer, they see me as an enemy. Of course they don't come out and say that, but their eyes give them away. They listen *at* me, not *to* me. They are actively passive right then, sitting there, waiting for the winds of change to dissipate. Their classmates have their number. They glance at the bully during our *Courage to Be Kind* presentation, but dare not make eye contact for fear of being attacked later. They are unrepentant serial bullies to whom kindness, compassion, and empathy are chump talk and to whom Protectors are pathetic "snitches who get stitches." Instead of coming clean, they dig their

71

heels in deeper and deeper into the psychological soil of their school, unwilling to yield an inch of power, domination, and control. They don't view their classmates as living cathedrals who emit the soft and veiled glow of the divine. They are commodities meant to be bartered and sold for popularity, entertainment, and sadistic pleasure.

When well-meaning Christian speakers repeat the convenient fallacy that the reason people bully others is because these bullies feel badly about themselves and have yet to discover their Golden You within (a highly humanistic view of human nature untethered from orthodox Christian belief), they are giving bullies the almighty "victim card," which bullies are more than happy play when called to make an account of their actions. These speakers are unintentionally giving bullies excuses for even more bad behavior. They need a stronger message. Bullies need confrontation that is grounded in both truth and love. They need the gift of desperation and objectivity about their real character, not so they wallow in shame and self-hatred but so that they too can be liberated.

These speakers unknowingly repeat the worldview, promoted by people like Carl Rogers, that our primary problem is that we don't love ourselves enough. This worldview, writes David Brooks, tells people they "don't need to combat themselves, they only need to open up, to liberate their inner selves, so that their internalized drive to self-actualize can take over. Self-love, self-praise, and self-acceptance are the paths to happiness."[5]

For the last sixty years, this nice message has blown into our culture, fundamentally changing how we assess ourselves and others, and creating havoc for an immeasurable number of tortured children, battered wives, sex slaves, and others dominated and abused by others. "This mindset is based on the romantic idea that each of us has a Golden Figure in the core of our self. There is an innately good True Self, which can be trusted."[6]

Many believe sin isn't found inside the soul of a person who has sinned. It's found out there, in society among racists and others who hate people for various reasons. Injustice is out there, not in here where their son's soul resides, because his soul is innately good and right, so he could never be a bully. To call him one isn't a nice thing to say, so it's forbidden. The path toward improvement is more self-love, not self-doubt, and certainly not more humility, which is for those who haven't learned to love themselves enough.

So the nice approach toward a bully, such as befriending him or her, is promoted as the only "Christian" option. We've helped many families create such a redemptive connection. But when we tell beleaguered targets and their families that playing nice is the only "Christian" option, we deal hope a body blow so powerful as to darken that family's future. It leaves millions of families with crushed eggs in only one battered basket. And when a child and parents or related guardians look into this basket of devastation, they will conclude that they have nowhere else to go. They might even conclude that God has forsaken them.

People like twenty-four-year-old Jennifer Martin, who now teaches at a Christian school in Pittsburgh, Pennsylvania, felt this way. She doesn't remember a time when she wasn't bullied in school for being overweight. Her parents, following a common "solution" found in many Christian circles, told her that her only option as a follower of Christ was to "kill the bullies with kindness" and show them "Christian compassion." Jennifer bought them bags of candy and told her bullies, especially Hannah, that she was praying for their souls. "Being nice to my bullies just made things worse for me," she says. They escalated their attacks, especially Hannah, who told Jennifer to kill herself, which wouldn't be a sin because she was a Christian and "God will forgive you."

Hannah, treating words as if they were spit, told Jennifer, "I don't want your prayers."

Targets and their families long for change—but without confrontation, as if that's possible. We don't change ourselves without confronting ourselves, yet for some reason we think this same dynamic isn't required when changing relationships with others. We help dozens of bullied children and their families each year. Yet sadly, when I tell them what really works to help them escape bullying, some don't like the answer. They want something nicer, and sometimes become noticeably upset with me. Some will say, "Don't you have a Christian answer?" To which I say, "I just gave it to you." In their minds, *Christian* means always gentle.

Instead, like Dorothy in the *Wizard of Oz*, they want to click their heels three times and make their problem go away. They rarely, if ever, change how they interact with their bullies, or the theater itself. They believe fate will magically save them, making it all go away. They will pray fervently for the bullying to stop, for God to "change the bully's heart," but not for the wisdom and courage needed to make the bullying stop, which is clearly part of God's plan for his children.

Our Lopsided Virtue

Environments have ecologies, and so do societies when it comes to morals, beliefs, norms, assumptions, and habits that have been handed down from generation to generation. This ecology, like air, water, and soil to a forest, creates a type of person, the way environmental ecologies create certain kinds of trees.

But moral ecologies do more than create. They favor certain attributes more than others. And for about a hundred years, wrote C. S. Lewis, "we have so concentrated on one of the virtues—'kindness.' . . . Such lopsided ethical developments are not uncommon, and other ages too have had their pet virtues and curious insensibilities."[7]

Kindness, the quality of being friendly, generous, and considerate, remains that lopsided virtue of our time. Our world needs more kindness, including the world of bullying. I'm proud to know Emily Davis, who is devoting her life to Beyond Kindness, a movement she created to help our nation be intentional about daily kindness, creating a heart and mindset of kindness that builds bridges among different people and restores relationships. But kindness alone won't foster the transformation needed to thwart bullying any more than "awareness" will—another buzzword in our culture, especially within education. And kindness, not to be mistaken for niceness, isn't the only virtue lauded in the Bible either. True, it is included in the verse of the Bible that we routinely recite when we talk about exemplary Christian behavior—"But the fruit of the Spirit is love, joy, peace, forbearance, kindness, goodness, faithfulness, gentleness and self-control" (Gal. 5:22–23 NIV)—but tougher virtues, what we might call the vegetables of the spirit, are also necessary if we are to possess integrity and godliness. These vegetable virtues demand that we possess a spectrum of behaviors and deeds, such as the ability to be both tender and tough, depending on the circumstances at hand. Author Brené Brown gives a rubber-meets-the-road definition of integrity when she says it's "putting courage before comfort."

Courage is also lauded in the Bible, a word that appears more than thirty times. And in Hebrews, we're admonished to not throw our courage away—implying that is what we do. Courage brings commitment, responsibility, and risk, so if we can throw courage away, we can get back to our undemanding lifestyles.

Kindness doesn't cure bullying just as penicillin doesn't cure cancer, because just as chemotherapy is needed to kill off the cancer, something needs to die within the bully as well. It can be ignorance, foolishness, or boredom, but more times than not, it's a more severe malady: besetting disdain, contempt, and predatory entitlement. The deeper the stain, the greater the solvent needed. Kindness without courage is like using Windex on a broken window—it doesn't fix the larger problem.

The theater of bullying needs tougher love from people who are both tender *and* tough, the way God is. "He has qualities both of austerity and of gentleness," wrote Martin Luther King Jr. "The Bible . . . expresses [God's] toughmindedness in his justice and wrath and his tenderheartedness in his love and grace."[8]

Church culture has the tender part down. The right kind of toughness, though—there's our problem.

Our Sinful Disease to Please (Even Bullies)

Because we don't have the corresponding toughness, our tenderness is too tender, creating spiritual veal with weak knees and backs. Having worked with tens of thousands of parents in Christian and public schools, I'm not convinced people want it any other way. When I ask parents how many want strong kids of character, achievement, and conviction, most every hand goes up. But when I ask how many want their child to experience pain, suffering, and hardship—the usual and traditional path toward greater character—they're dismayed. Unlike past generations, they don't believe there's a connection between hardship and character. They don't really believe that saying no on behalf of themselves and others is one of the greatest spiritual words they and their children can say.

Instead of rearing good kids, we have settled for nice kids who are infected with the disease to please others, even serial bullies. Writer Naomi Shulman went viral when she wrote this shocking statement about niceness, the greatest compliment you can give someone inside and outside church today:

Nice people made the best Nazis.

Or so I have been told. My mother was born in Munich in 1934, and spent her childhood in Nazi Germany surrounded by nice people who refused to make waves. When things got ugly, the people my mother lived alongside chose not to focus on "politics," instead busying themselves with happier things. They were lovely, kind people who turned their heads as their neighbors were dragged away. . . . You know who weren't nice people? Resisters.[9]

Shulman reminds me about my time in high school when I stood up for a boy with Down syndrome who was being bullied by Greg, who was bigger than me, a wrestler, and a jerk. We had finished gym class, and back then, taking a shower was compulsory. So most took a shower as quickly as they could, got to their lockers, changed, and ran off to their next class. It was a near perfect environment for bullying to thrive because students had to be there, they were physically and psychologically vulnerable, targets had their backs turned, there was no real supervision, lockers blocked the line-of sight needed for authority to know what was happening, and students were also under a strong time-lock. Criminals look for a similar dynamic.

Targets were sitting ducks, and bullies knew it.

Greg called this large, mute boy horrible and disgusting names. He made filthy comments about his mother, who I'm confident Greg never even met. The boy with Down syndrome, who was standing right next to me, started crying. His shoulders heaved. I wasn't a Christian then, but I knew students who were. Some were in that locker room at the very same time. They saw what I saw, felt great pity and sorrow for this young man whom none of us really knew. But not one of the openly Christian young men stood up for him. They, too, turned their heads. Said nothing. Did nothing. They turned their heads *because they were nice instead of good*. If people are not compelled to stem the psychological torment of another person when it's within their power to act, does God's Spirit really live within them?

Niceness was once synonymous with "ignorant," "dainty," and "unable to endure." It is almost always a knee-jerk reaction to please others, avoid conflict at all cost, and keep our bubble of comfort, security, and certainty snag-free. It's not in the same category as goodness, not even close. Nor should it be viewed as synonymous with kindness. Niceness is too often our spiritual security blanket, designed to keep the Big Bad World at bay. The problem is that this security blanket only keeps you warm on easy summer nights, not in the difficult fall and surely not in the hard winter when the angry winds, like bullying, howl.

To be truly kind, we must sometimes disagree and create conflict with other people, such as sexual harassers, which requires courage. Some kind people have this capacity for righteousness. Nice people, however, don't possess such strength, though they are glad to give others the impression that they do. Many are in the sticky grip of cowardice, which is listed in the Bible as a sin—right up there with adultery, lying, thievery, and sorcery (Rev. 21:8). If courage is our foundational virtue, as mentioned earlier, could it be that its opposite, cowardice, is the foundational vice upon which all other vices receive their underlying power? Is it cowardice, for example, that really keeps more Christians from becoming missionaries? This question is worthy of deep consideration and exploration from within the church and related institutions if we're serious about doing more than just avoiding sin—instead being genuine salt, light, courage, and righteousness in the world.

Niceness is sometimes cowardice masquerading as spiritual maturity. It's a defensive and fear-encrusted orientation toward life.

It's better than being mean, but not by much, especially as it relates to how we respond to bullying. Niceness doesn't prepare children like Alex Moore for the Lord-of-the-Flies world of adolescence. Yet niceness remains one of the top pet virtues of our time.

Alex Moore lived in an R-rated world, yet we adults insist it is PG through our clarion calls for decency and kindness from people who aren't decent or kind. Abuse expert and expert witness in sexual abuse cases Dr. Anna Salter tells us one of the main reasons why: "Normal, healthy people distort reality to create a kinder, gentler world than actually exists."[10] This is the philosophical underpinning that keeps our Niceness Doctrine alive, harming children in uncountable ways.

Past and Present Abuser Myths

When abuse is viewed through nice, grace-tinted lenses, we sometimes don't recognize the behavior for what it is and are prone to see what we want to see. We thought this way about sexual predators at one time. Like the grave findings of Dr. Milgram, we couldn't believe people would be so deliberately diabolical, so, as we do with bullies, we adhered to a slew of myths instead. We once believed that if we really wanted to keep our children safe from sexual predators, we needed to keep an eagle eye on strangers. In fact, most sexual assaults are committed by someone known to the victim or the victim's family.

More to the point in regard to bullying, many still believe that children who are sexually assaulted will grow up to sexually assault others as a way of ridding themselves of the shame they harbor deep inside. The fact is, most sexually assaulted children do *not* grow up to assault others, just as most kids who are bullied don't become bullies. While past sexual victimization can increase the likelihood of sexually aggressive behavior (we have reason to believe that around 30 percent of sexual predators were sexually abused as children), most people who were sexually victimized as children never perpetrate against others.

Like bullying, sexual predation is actually a crime of practice and habit, not opportunity. Both plan their assaults ahead of time, often modifying their lives around their desire to abuse others with cold-hearted and calculated precision. Though we cannot label all serial bullies as psychopaths, we can label many if not all of them as *almost psychopaths*. Ronald Schouten, MD, and James Silver, JD, wrote one of the most helpful but least recognized resources for how to understand the mind and nature of a serial bully. In *Almost a Psychopath*, they write about the "almost effect," which describes how dangerous predators don't exhibit all the characteristics of a condition, yet still have enough to be exceedingly dangerous. And because they don't carry an official label, we underestimate their destructive power.

Such people

- engage in reactive and instrumental aggression, where aggression is predatory and preplanned (also called "proactive aggression");
- are superficial, glib, and charming;
- act friendly to get what they want but don't commit actual acts of friendship;
- are dangerous even when showing a pleasant demeanor.[11]

Niceness Doesn't Set Captives Free

The oppressed don't always wear handcuffs. Their ankles aren't always bruised and purpled from shackles. Alex Moore was one of the captives Jesus came to liberate, but who chose a severe and desperate path to liberation. Yet many don't think she was a true captive. They believe she had viable choices all along the way. *Leave school* (even though it's compulsory). *Tell those bullies to stop enough times, and they will. Appeal to their innate good-ness and befriend them. Tell them how you really feel so it will melt their hearts. Love them even more. Avoid them. Ignore them. Pity them. Take the high road. Love Jesus more; then watch your need for their approval grow strangely dim. Pray, and God will deliver you. Whatever you do, don't bully the bully.* These are all choices, but most are false choices within a system and youth culture that favors bullies. Without some form of intervention, Alex Moore was destined for more psychological trauma.

We don't have this same attitude toward those captive to sex trafficking, the cause *du jour* of our time within the church. We don't say that these women have choices, the way we do about bullied children, whose numbers are far greater than those in sex trafficking. We don't say, "It's not like these young ladies are hand-cuffed all the time. Why don't they plan their getaway and walk out the door when no one is looking? Sneak out at night?"

And we would certainly never say to them what we say to bul-lied children: "Just have a heart-to-heart with him. Tell him how you really feel and it will change his heart. And if he slaps you on the face, turn your face so he can slap the other side. If he steals your money again, give him double. If he makes you sleep with one, sleep with two. This way you will win him to Christ."

Interestingly, we don't hold our battle against human traffick-ing to the demands of the Niceness Doctrine. When police across the globe raid the dens of human traffickers, they don't bust in with a bouquet of nice flowers in their hands or Bible verses on their lips. They bring guns and yell non-negotiable demands.

We're willing to believe in the psychological captivity of a girl or woman caught in the terror-soaked web of sex trafficking some-where across the globe, or in a big city in America, but not the psychological captivity of a target of bullying on our own block. There is no crime admitting this—but there is a moral crime if we accept this fallacy. And when we ponder how many more targets of ongoing bullying there really are throughout the world compared with those in human trafficking, we perceive just how great the chasm is between how the world is and *shalom*—the way things ought to be. A veil lifts and we realize that our God is so big that we can play our part in helping both. Scales fall from the eyes of those who possess a more courageous faith that allows them not to just be in the presence of a more intimate injustice, but to be a penetrating solvent, like salt and like light, to combat it. We realize that we don't have to go to Uganda or Bangladesh or other dens of iniquity in order to be the hands and heart of God. We can be even larger and more splendid peacemakers right now, today, in our own neighborhood. The money that would go into traveling other there can be donated to your local school to help support and sustain anti-bullying efforts. We can also burn out the bad soil contaminated by our own behavior since many of us have been complicit bystanders and even bullies at one time or another. We may not be able to make amends with our targets, but we can help future targets.

Because Alex Moore is everywhere. She's the child in your beloved community where your children or neighbor's children or your future children or grandchildren play, and she needs mountains of love to do well in life. She shakes under sheets at night, just like that little girl who is sex trafficked in Bangladesh or Atlanta. She also has the storm clouds of hopelessness and rage forming in her young soul and tender spirit. She also questions God's existence. And if he does exist, is he just? She also asks at night, *Are those who claim to represent God just? Because I go to school with them and I hear them talk about God, but when they see what those kids do to me, not only do they not help me; they laugh along with everyone else.*

Like those enslaved to human trafficking, what Alex Moore and the tens of millions she represents need isn't a nice or even kind shoulder to cry on. Not ultimately. What they need is a student of conviction and leadership born from a courageous heart and faith. They need a real woman or a real man of good character with sturdy shoulders to stand on. Someone with guts who knows just how redemptive, powerful, and spiritual the word no really is. Good people stand up while nice people . . . do nothing meaningful. Sure they wring their hands and say how awful things are. But they don't act. They don't do. As author Bob Goff reminds us, *Love does.*

We currently act and speak as if Jesus said that the greatest expression of love is for a person to be nice to a friend, knowing that what he really said was for a person to lay down his or her life for a friend (John 15:13). I think this can be literal or figurative; but either way, it's deeply sacrificial. It costs us far more than niceness does, which is probably the reason we cherish niceness so much. It looks and feels delightful, but without the demanding side effects of hardship and difficulty. The right thing and the hard thing are almost always the same thing. Niceness doesn't have enough horsepower to compel us through this aphorism and into the benefits of spiritual maturing and ripening. But courageous love does. Pastor Pete Kelley put it this way: "It could be that our greatest sin is our refusal to sacrifice, to take a chance."

An attorney asked if I would help his client, a poor Mexican-American immigrant daughter and her mother. I took the case for free in part because my parents were immigrants and I have a soft spot for underdogs. But I took the case for a larger reason. Her daughter was so brutally bullied that her mother had her under suicide watch. She made her daughter sleep in her bed for more than three months, many times within her anxious clutch. The sweet, quiet mother with a beautiful accent was traumatized as well. She cried many times during our meeting and begged for help. Then I asked her the names of the school officials to whom she went for help. I knew one of them.

"What did he do for your daughter?" I asked.

"He was very nice. But he didn't help us," she said.

She didn't have to tell me. My gut already knew that this nice and pleasant man who went to church would be of no real help. Nice people rarely are. I stayed with the case for free because I know that not only does niceness not lead to goodness, it is responsible for untold miscarriages of justice, as was the case for this poor immigrant girl who had already tried to take her life and for her humble mother who feared she would swallow those pills again.

Notes

[1] Thomas Blass, *The Man Who Shocked the World: The Life and Legacy of Stanley Milgram* (New York: Basic Books, 2009), iBooks.

[2] Blass, *The Man Who Shocked the World*, iBooks.

[3] Blass, *The Man Who Shocked the World*, iBooks.

[4] R. T. France, "Matthew," in *New Bible Commentary: 21st Century Edition*, ed. Gordon J. Wenham, J. A. Motyer, D. A. Carson, R. T. France (Leicester, UK: InterVarsity Press, 1994), 912.

[5] David Brooks, *The Road to Character* (New York: Random House, 2015), iBooks.

[6] Brooks, *The Road to Character*, iBooks.

[7] C. S. Lewis, *A Year with C. S. Lewis: Daily Readings from His Classic Works* (New York: HarperCollins, 2003), 282.

[8] Martin Luther King Jr., *A Gift of Love: Sermons from* Strength to Love *and Other Preachings* (Boston: Beacon Press, 2015), 8.

[9] Naomi Shulman, "No Time to Be Nice: Now Is Not the Moment to Remain Silent," *Cognoscenti: Thinking That Matters* (blog), WBUR (November 17, 2016), http://www.wbur.org/cognoscenti/2016/11/17/the-post -election-case-for-speaking-out-naomi-shulman.

[10] Anna Salter, *Predators: Pedophiles, Rapists and Other Sex Offenders: Who They Are, How They Operate, and How We Can Protect Ourselves and Our Children* (New York: Basic Books 2003), 177.

[11] Ronald Schouten and James Silver, *Almost a Psychopath: Do I (or Does Someone I Know) Have a Problem with Manipulation and Lack of Empathy?* (Center City, MN: Hazelden, 2012).

Three Divine Protectors

Two remarkable, young men and one amazing, young woman changed the life of Mark Earwood's son Cyle forever. Each appeared at a time when Cyle was vulnerable and an easy target for bullying. In Mark's words, "I believe they saved him."

When he was five years old, Cyle was diagnosed with Pervasive Developmental Disorder on the autism spectrum. And after witnessing the cruelty and bullying Cyle endured at the first school he attended, Mark and his wife moved Cyle to a private Christian school.

One day, Mark intended to surprise Cyle at school with his favorite cheeseburger and Dr. Pepper for lunch. Mark was about to enter the cafeteria when he saw Cyle through the glass door. Cyle had already gone through the lunch line and was walking toward the last seat available at a table of his classmates.

"I saw him sit down with a big smile on his face," Mark said. "Then one of the girls looked at him with a 'how dare you' glare and then leaned over and said something to the other girls. They got up simultaneously and moved to another table. Cyle's smile disappeared, and he escaped into his autism, blocking out the pain of what he just experienced."

His autism often caused him to stuff his mouth with food, and he had difficulty feeling his face. "The mess he made was extreme, but the cruelty, ridicule, and isolation heaped upon him by his classmates was more than my wife and I could bear."

Mark and his wife, like many parents, began to wonder if placing their son in a private Christian school was going to be any better for him than the public school he had left.

That's when Jacob came along. He was a senior and a great football player, standing over six foot four and weighing around 250 pounds. Jacob had time in his class schedule to volunteer in a special needs classroom, where he and Cyle struck up an amazing friendship. Jacob regularly passed on the privilege of leaving campus for lunch with his senior classmates. Instead, Jacob chose to eat with Cyle so that he wouldn't have to eat alone. "Jacob laughed with Cyle and gently instructed and corrected him, which made others view him as more than just the odd kid who was a messy eater," Mark said. Jacob told others of Cyle's sharp sense of humor and urged them to get to know Cyle better.

When Jacob graduated, it left a void of companionship and protection, which resurrected a fear in the Earwood household. "Lord, who will take his place?" they asked.

Then Zach came along.

He was in Cyle's grade and was among the most popular boys, not because of his stature or other external attributes but because Zach had an easy way about him that others admired. He was outgoing, engaging, and charismatic.

Zach took Cyle under his wing and included him in almost all of the on-campus and off-campus outings. He made it cool to include Cyle. But Cyle was not universally accepted. Mark says,

"There were a few young men who didn't like having him around and were easily annoyed by him. Zach knew this and made it clear that if Cyle couldn't come, Zach wasn't coming either." This stand was put the test more than once, according to Mark, and Zach remained true to his word. Zach is now an officer in the U.S. Army, still protecting the innocent.

Cyle's third protector was Jordan. She was known as the prettiest girl on campus, possibly the smartest, and to this day is still the most accomplished female athlete her school has ever enrolled. Jordan is an outstanding young woman who chose to spend her social capital on Cyle. "She was considered off-limits by most guys because she was so accomplished and almost intimidating," Mark says. "She was Cyle's classmate and was on the track team with him as well. She was always very sweet and patient with him—never unkind."

But, that didn't mean that bullies stopped taking shots at Cyle, who during his junior year was pressured by a group of boys to ask a girl to prom. Cyle, not realizing the ulterior motive of bullies, or their fiend friendship, followed through and asked a young lady if she would be his date. She told him that she didn't think she was going to go to prom that year and declined. Cyle took it well until he found out that the same girl said yes to the next boy who asked.

"Cyle is autistic, not stupid," Mark says. "Autism is not about intelligence. It's about processing and the lack of innate social skills, like the ability to read people and sense when something should be said or not said. Cyle feels what everyone else feels. He just can't express it by normal or innate means. This is why many kids with undiagnosed autism are labeled 'weird' by their peers. Many function just fine in academics. But it's personal relationships, social skills, and emotional expression where they struggle. That's Cyle. He could deduce what her rejection of him and acceptance of another meant. What he didn't know how to do was handle it emotionally."

When he found out, Cyle told Mark, "She really did want to go to prom. She just didn't want to go with me." This raw revelation broke Mark's heart. So, you can only imagine Mark's astonishment when word swept across the campus that Cyle had asked Jordan to prom! "Jordan's parents are dear friends of mine, so I called her mom to talk about ways that Jordan could politely decline without hurting Cyle. When her mom relayed my call to Jordan, she said, 'Well, that settles it. I'm saying yes.'" She told her mother and Mark that she felt God wanted her to go with Cyle so that he could experience an event that other high schoolers get to experience.

Almost nine years later, Jordan and Cyle are still dear friends.

Like most other protectors, Jordan is humble about her good deeds and truthful about her character. "Mark sees me with rose-colored glasses," she said. "I don't see myself like that at all. I was not perfect. I would sometimes get irritated with Cyle. Sometimes he would squeeze me too hard, which hurt, so I had to tell him to give me some space. But living a loving life isn't about being perfect; it's choosing to be kind regularly."

Another trait that Jordan shares with other protectors is that she knows what it's like to be marginalized. "I felt like an outcast as well. I was really shy in middle school. I couldn't talk to a boy without freaking out. I know what it's like to feel lonely." Yet at the same time, she said, "I truly believe that Christ empowers us to do things that are outside of our character. So, even though I was shy, I stuck up for Cyle. Because of our friendship, some boys would tease Cyle by encouraging him to ask me to marry him while we were in middle school. I'd have to say things like, 'Cyle, you know we're too young to get married.'" Jordan says it took more courage than she naturally had to push back against her classmates. "The bravest thing you can do is to be kind. It's not about making big, heroic stands. It's about doing the small, kind things regularly at school."

Jordan paid a price for being friends with Cyle. "Sometimes doing the right thing is thankless, just like the Bible says. I felt misunderstood by my classmates. When I went to prom with Cyle, I remember having to help him wipe spaghetti off his face because he couldn't feel his face. My classmates noticed these things, and it made them uncomfortable. Because I danced with Cyle, no other boy would ask me to dance." But her classmates were not the only ones who noticed her actions. "Teachers and other adults respected what I did. I even got letters from adults who thanked me. I felt mature during those moments."

While Mark believes that Cyle's protectors saved him, Jordan believes it is the other way around. "Cyle saved us," she said. "He is one of the most genuine, honest, and lovable people you could know. He's the definition of a true and loyal friend. He would call me or text me while I was in college to say that he was praying for me. Other friends didn't do that. It wasn't a huge sacrifice going to prom with Cyle. The bullies only saw his weaknesses, and they attacked him for that. I saw his strengths, and I've been blessed."

CHAPTER FIVE

Justice-Minded Children Have More Courage and Success

> *Woe to him whom this world charms from Gospel duty!*
> —Father Mapple, *Moby Dick*

> *I tremble for my country when I reflect that God is just, that his justice cannot sleep forever.* —Thomas Jefferson

WHEN IT COMES TO THE JUDEO-CHRISTIAN GOD AND THE TOPIC OF JUSTICE, THERE ARE OFTEN TWO CHURCH CAMPS that perceive one another warily. On one side is a minority who needs no convincing. They are more kingdom minded than church minded people, who seem to be born with a powerful drive to see justice done. Many have been bitten by injustice at a tender age, creating an acute and even hyper-reaction to injustices done to themselves and others.

The other camp is larger and composed of people who are more church minded than kingdom minded. They have experienced injustice, but they seem to not empathize with the injustice of others with the same frequency and intensity as their more kingdom-minded counterparts. Both are members of the same body that comprises the church. There is ignorance, misunderstanding, and even prejudice on both sides. Both read the same Bible, but they read it differently. Both go to the same church, yet they view the mission of the church differently, as well. Howard Snyder explains the differences between the two groups this way:

> Kingdom people seek first the Kingdom of God and its justice; church people often put church work above concerns of justice, mercy and truth. Church people think about how to get people into the church; Kingdom people think about how to get the church into the world. Church people worry that the world might change the church; Kingdom people work to see the church change the world.[1]

It is my hope with this chapter to bring reconciliation between these two groups—to bridge the current chasm to the glory of God, to the spiritual maturation of his people—and to rescue millions of bullied children throughout the world.

One mistake the justice-minded make is to hurl Bible verses and statements from respected thinkers at others within the body of Christ. For example, they'll tell those who are not justice minded that the Bible says God does not want to hear our worship unless justice is present among us. They quote Amos 5:23–24:

> Take away from Me the noise of your songs;
>   I will not even listen to the sound of your harps.
> But let justice roll down like waters
>   And righteousness like an ever-flowing stream. (NASB)

The justice-minded think this is airtight, that there cannot be any argument as to the deep truth of God's will that his people labor on behalf of justice. Their hopes are soon crushed because the church-minded will often let their eyes skate across the word *justice* but stop upon the word *righteousness*, which they define as the avoidance of sin. Also, the church-minded will observe the lifestyles of justice-minded Christians and complain that they don't care enough about the avoidance of sin. Their complaint has merit. There are sins of commission and omission on both sides of the spiritual aisle. It's my hope that we can care deeply about both justice and the avoidance of sin in our lives. Jesus talked about something similar when he said, "Woe to you, scribes and Pharisees, hypocrites! For you tithe . . . and have neglected the weightier provisions of the law: justice and mercy and faithfulness; but these are the things you should have done without neglecting the others" (Matt. 23:23 NASB). Jesus didn't say that they shouldn't have paid such close attention to the religious practice, only that they neglected the weightier matters that God cares deeply about.

Having hurled a few Bible verses myself about the importance of justice only to witness them fall hard to the pretty sanctuary carpet to later be trampled upon, I've seen how ineffective this can be. It usually becomes only a mental exercise, and doesn't move us into committing new acts of life-giving aid to others, nor does it lead to the faith-growing experience that God wills for his children. Most of the time, people just dig their heels into the thinking of their past since justice can be such a provocative and sometimes guilt-producing topic.

We need a fresh approach toward justice-minded Christianity, and I hope to provide it here through an intimate and somewhat provocative means—by describing the character of a Christian who did not have the influence of justice thinking and living in his spiritual formation.

I'm qualified to describe this kind of person because I was one. So I'm going to tell you what it did to me, how it influenced others, and what it's doing right now to people, especially during their spiritually formative years.

Starting in my teens, I attended a string of churches where church leaders would mention but not expand upon Bible verses that called for the creation of justice, even in churches that claimed to go through the Bible "chapter by chapter, verse by verse." Instead, they taught on other words in the Bible passages that advocated justice. These other words and concepts that surrounded justice always came first, even when they weren't the primary topic the verses addressed. These other concepts were almost always matters of personal morality. We didn't have guest speakers talk about justice either. Looking back, they would not have been welcome. When needs were mentioned, it was only the needs of those inside our church.

I was taught that Jesus did not come to bring "justice" to the nations. He came to bring righteousness, the ability to overcome sin.

I was taught that the rich Hebrew concept of *shalom* was really a one-dimensional and callow belief in personal peace only, as opposed to the biblical understanding of corporate well-being that includes the guiding principles of justice and fairness for all.

One of my pastors was especially gifted at ridiculing Christians who emphasized justice as part of their spiritual formation and faith in Jesus. He did so with a smile on his face and a lilt in his winsome voice, making his ridicules harder to spot. He and his elders portrayed such people as being gullible, second-class Christians who rearranged the furniture on a sinking cruise liner during these "End Times." They believed that real, "Spirit-filled" Christians didn't concern themselves with such "worldly" matters when saving souls was all that mattered. Christians who labored on behalf of justice weren't listening or following the leadership of the Holy Spirit. They actually went against the deeper will of God.

Think for a moment how attractive such a message is to a person and to a family. God doesn't require you to labor on behalf of others, especially the vulnerable, which can be arduous, messy, and risky. Being salt and light really means scrubbing your life of sin, going to church, proselytizing, and tithing. This requires some sacrifice, but not much, if any, conflict. To more mild people who already feel overwhelmed by life, especially when starting a family, this is no small attraction.

A steady drip of this teaching, especially delivered with ether-like charisma, altered my spiritual DNA. I became a different kind of person, and I didn't like what I was seeing.

I became more glib and cavalier, especially toward the suffering of others. My spiritual transformation was bolstered by another negative attribute—robotic smugness. I began to see myself as special, the way our pastor believed that he and his family were special. I began to behave as if I had arrived. Sure, there was more spiritual growth to be had by scrubbing my life of sin; but other than that, there were no more spiritual hills to climb. There wasn't community involvement, other than going to church and attending fellowship groups where, looking back, there was a discernible lack of honesty and authenticity. Appearance was far more important than authentic connection, a reflection of the leadership. We certainly weren't concerned about people in need. We were what some call the "Holy Huddle"—salvation-only Christians who had found the keys to the kingdom, the *only* set of keys to the kingdom. If I had to choose one word to describe what was happening to me, it would be *leaching*. Qualities and characteristics that make us more loving and mature were leaving me, though I didn't recognize it at first.

What we did and didn't value was sometimes mystifying. Even though Jesus expressed plenty of indignation over the injustices he saw, I only witnessed our pastor's indignation when the county wouldn't allow the church to build another building on an already large campus. He spoke as if the use of force was always wrong—until it came to spanking a defenseless child. Though Jesus was incredibly heroic in his courageous denunciations against those who were leading others astray, I was floored when one pastor admonished a packed sanctuary, "Don't do anything heroic."

All of us operate with presuppositions, tacit assumptions that are largely unstated as we speak or take a course of action. One of the presuppositions we have when going to church is what we expect to get. Do we go to church to be healed from spiritual maladies, the way we go to a hospital, and then expect on the other side of treatment to grow in strength and bless others with our strength? Or do we go to church to escape the world, like going into a nursery, which is run by nice and kind people and designed not to heal but merely to alleviate discomfort? Do we go to be healed so we can heal and bless others, sometimes through performing acts of loving justice? Or do we really go to escape and flee the Big Bad World for a few hours, like going to a really good movie?

If God's will for the church is to be more like a nursery than a hospital, then the church experiences I just described are appropriate because nothing more is needed. More would be overkill. But I think you will join me in believing that the nursery model is more than wrong. It makes you feel kind of sick inside because it's so childish. C. S. Lewis believed that there is a real and predatory evil in this world that longs to harm and destroy. Because of this reality, the church should be attentive and listening for our secret message like an operative awaiting instructions during wartime. The church is where, or should be where, we receive our marching orders from our commanding officer in a kind of revolution against the evil forces on this earth. Because we live in an enemy occupied territory, we really need a physician, not a wet nurse; a hospital, not a nursery.

I challenge anyone who doesn't believe in evil and wickedness to study the real world of adolescent bullying for even a few days. At the very least, it will challenge the presupposition that people are innately good, especially when they weigh prevalent and unvarnished bystander apathy. And many will come to believe in evil, though they might steer clear of any and all religious connotation, which they may consider akin to superstition. My devotion to helping targets of bullying left me no alternative but to confirm the existence and nature of evil and its crushing influence upon the vulnerable, which is a blue-collar definition of injustice. This revelation of real evil and God's mandate to combat it, more than any other, caused me to reject the kind of Christianity that harmed my spiritual growth and the growth of others.

It's embarrassing to admit these faults in my character; yet in my own defense, I didn't know any better. I had no other discernible points on my compass. What I did have was a nagging disquietude—glimpses into the reality that what I was told and what I was doing were really fancy gyrations in missing the point. I now have many other points on my compass having spoken to close to a hundred churches throughout the world. And also in my own defense, I chafed pretty quickly. I saw in myself what I saw in other "true believers," and I was repulsed. I was growing smaller and smaller, though I was told I was growing bigger and bigger.

I was becoming a mile wide and an inch deep. All hat. No cattle. I was growing in knowledge of God but not of his guiding wisdom nor life-giving love, courage, and strength. I was becoming what Paul wrote about: a noisy gong, full of opinions but untethered from love, the driving force of life.

By contrast, when I began to labor on behalf of justice, it did more than stem this leaching. It put needed nutrients back into my spiritual soil. I learned how to endure suffering better, to be calmer in the face of difficulty. To lean into God more during these times and become more grateful. I experienced moments of grace and blessings, especially during times of financial need. I experienced the joy of helping set others free. And because I had become a true peacemaker, Jesus told me that I am now called a child of God. I don't know all that this means, but I'm sure it's larger and more splendid than my imagination can contain.

Justice ministry helped remove the fear I had of relating to others, thinking I had to somehow fix everything, and know all the right answers. I learned better how to "hold space," to be with people in pain and suffering and just be with them. That process alone blesses others and myself, but I wouldn't have known this if it weren't for the portal of justice.

I grew in wisdom—the ability to apply knowledge in a complex situation—which helped battle a naivety. I had a lot of perfect-world thinking, given to me in part through reductionist sermons that damaged my faith. I annexed needed skepticism (not to be mistaken for cynicism) into my understanding of life. I became much better at spotting dissimulation and related behaviors, helping me, and others, avoid needless pain and suffering.

I became better at repelling nefarious people, and helping others repel them as well, including many pastors who would have walked away from their sacred vocation without such needed wisdom. I studied the ways of the wicked, who carry within themselves the seed of their own undoing. I helped others speed up this process in order to liberate the innocent.

Having spoken to tens of thousands of students, and trained thousands of parents, teachers, coaches, and others who work with youth to diminish adolescent bullying, I have helped make this world a better place, and this good work cannot be undone.

But I wouldn't have grown in my faith and love, and I would not have this level of meaning and purpose in my life, if I hadn't woken up and adopted a more biblical view of life, and the character needed to thrive within it. I want my children to care about justice because I want them to be whole. I want them to be balanced and possess discernible integrity. And I want this for you and your children. I want, during my limited time on this planet, to manage the soil of my life in such a way that I get the most out of it. I don't want to miss out on what God has for me as part of his beloved creation.

Helping, protecting, and even rescuing others who are incapable of self-rescue is messy and disruptive. Sometimes you don't know what to say or what to do. It really does a number on our comfortable, sugar-water life and religion. But as I experienced, that life leads to spiritual cavities. I saw it in the lives of my college friends who grew up on a steady diet of spiritual training that, like mine, ignored the weightier matters of God. Few remain in the faith today. They just weren't very deep religiously. At least, not deep enough to remain tethered to the faith when the winds of life and modernity hit. They didn't bite into meaty causes and actions, which would have in turn made them meatier and stronger. Their detached, safe, me-centered, and robotic "Holy Huddle" insured a small and purpose-bleeding life. It's a security blanket we all want to hold, but it's a forbidden one because it doesn't lead to faith and it doesn't lead to life.

Do We Really Want Strong Children?

Parents, do you want strong children? My adolescent friends, do you really want to be strong? Of course you do. But these questions don't get to the soul of the matter: How does one become strong? Prayer, church attendance, and regular Bible study aid strength, the way sunshine helps a magnolia grow. But it takes another nutrient, and that nutrient is courage, which is only grown by committing courageous acts, such as standing up to bullying.

Courage and strength go hand-in-hand in life and in the Bible. The sign for courage Sign Language is touching your chest with both hands (where our thumotic courage resides) and then making two clenched fists. And in the Bible, the two words are nearly synonymous, often appearing in the same sentence or same paragraph, such as in Joshua 1:6 and 1 Corinthians 16:13. Biblical courage is committing acts of bravery and strength that are tethered to wisdom (courage without wisdom is foolhardy) as well as faith. Strong and courageous people say no to what is bad for them and others. Courageous people don't watch others suffer and offer no help when it's within their power to act. Courageous people resist what's wrong much in the same way athletes resist weights because the results are similar: strength, one being moral and spiritual strength; the other being physical strength. Strength is the fruit of courage when we resist what God wants us to resist.

But then some of us receive a peculiar religious (some seminary-trained pastors I know call it "heretical") training that says, "Don't bother." This training either doesn't talk about God's will for justice, or if it does, it changes the meaning of words and even ridicules those who follow their God-given conscience about right and wrong. These churches have teachers and preachers who quote this most famous passage from the prophet Micah: "He has shown you, O mortal, what is good. And what does the LORD require of you? To act justly and to love mercy and to walk humbly with your God" (6:8 NIV).

Yet they only expound upon the virtues of mercy and humility. They leave acts of justice behind. They preach only two-thirds of its content, intentionally. They are prejudiced against justice, part of the very character of God.

As children, more than 90 percent of us start life believing in the self-evident nature and existence of God. Then as we grow older, we lose our belief. For most, it doesn't happen right away.

Most don't sit down and reason their way away from God. It's a loss of faith and belief by a thousand letdowns. The vast majority of these stabbings involve injustices both big and small. People look at the world in which they live and conclude, usually quietly and to themselves, that this God of love and justice just doesn't exist.

Though *justice* outpaces *forgiveness* in appearances in the Bible by thirteen to one, we still talk far more about forgiveness. I hope this ratio is seen as obvious proof as to how out of balance we are, and how a lack of balance brings with it a flimsy integrity that is not incidental. Blessed are those who forgive, and blessed are those who create actual peace.

The people who lose their belief in God, such as targets of bullying, see self-professed Christians turn a blind eye to injustice. So, these targets get a double-dose of disbelief. They are told that the God of the Universe is love, but they are attacked and abused regularly. Then they are told that Christians represent this God of love, yet they are as unlikely to offer any help than other bystanders. Our lack of courage plays a role in their unbelief.

I'm reminded of Monica, that bright tenth grade girl I spoke with in California. After our *Courage to be Kind* presentation, she told me about how she had been bullied for years in that private Christian school by a group of girls who went to the same church. Her faith seemed to be able to absorb this truth. But what she could not surmount was how her friends not only did not support or defend her; they at times joined the mean girls. Most of these friends went to the same church as well. That broke her faith. She's an atheist today for this one reason, she said. She no longer goes to church, though the rest of her family does. The sin of cowardice from her so-called friends helped create a ripple effect that ruptured tight family bonds. Such is the life-stealing nature of sin since withholding justice from the wounded in spirit is like withholding food from the homeless and hungry. Justice is a God-created human expectation.

Though we all grow older, not all of us really mature. We usually don't notice this until it's pointed out. For example, we think that someone has grown in kindness. But what has really happened is that the once cantankerous and bullying family member is just running out of energy, so they appear kinder and more agreeable. We mistake decay for decency, and loss of energy for peacefulness. I highlight this truth because the spiritual maturity we want for ourselves and our children isn't built into the system of our lives. Though we naturally run out of energy, we don't naturally grow up. We gravitate toward comfort and fear, not courage, so some form of force, not coercion, is required for growth. The force of justice ministry, beginning at a younger age, aids our need for life-long growth that leads to deep and abiding faith, love, and hope.

When I tell Alex Moore's story across the country, numerous people are moved to tears. That may include you right now. You may feel sorrow for shy Alex, and you never even met her. But unless our sorrow moves us to action and resolve, our sorrow remains about us, not the millions of children who undergo what Alex had to go through each school day. Tears and grief must lead us to more than sorrow, important as that is, because as Betty Williams, the 1976 Nobel Laureate for Peace has noted, "Tears without action are wasted sentiment." They must lead us to indignation, a driving force for change. If they don't, not only will more children become the walking wounded that we see among us as adults, but something within us dies as well. We are mysteriously linked, for good or bad, to the suffering of others. When we don't act, we harm ourselves. Martin Luther King Jr. described this dynamic this way:

You may be thirty-eight years old, as I happen to be.
And one day, some great opportunity stands before you
and calls you to stand up for some great principle, some
great issue, some great cause. And you refuse to do it
because you are afraid . . . that you will be criticized or
that you will lose your popularity . . . so you refuse to
take the stand.

Well, you may go on and live until you are ninety, but
you're just as dead at thirty-eight as you would be at ninety.
And the cessation of breathing in your life is but the
belated announcement of an earlier death of the spirit.[2]

There is a way out through this bramble of hate—but we will have to honor the voice speaking to us right now through our conscience, and God's Holy Spirit, that tells us, *Do more than cry*. It compels us to roll up our sleeves and join arms to spend time, treasure, and talent in what is our most under-recognized mission field.

And when we join this hallowed call, we become better, stronger, more magnanimous souls as well. That's because though bullying represents the worst in human nature, combatting it represents the best. And we can be sure that God is on our side. There are mysteries about God that we may never know this side of eternity. But his love for justice isn't one of them.

A great and even eternal opportunity stands before us right now as a people of faith and other people of goodwill. Join this movement to harness our tears, sorrow, grief, and indignation into a laser of love and liberation for the broken and oppressed within our homes and neighborhoods—the exact group that the major to minor Hebrew prophets, from Isaiah to Malachi, admonished us to help. Jesus continued their cry to liberate the wounded and poor in spirit when he proclaimed: "The Spirit of the Lord is upon me, because he has chosen me to bring good news to the poor. He has sent me to proclaim liberty to the captives and recovery of sight to the blind, to set free the oppressed" (Luke 4:18 GNT).

Second Seed People

Weightier endeavors, such as creating justice, imbue us with more character than we would have otherwise. And as Jesus taught in the Parable of the Sower (so important that it's listed in three of the four Gospels), they can even help keep us from losing our faith.

Jesus attracted such a gigantic crowd that he had to get on a boat in order to face the masses that had gathered on the shore. He provided in detail three different metaphors revolving around the kingdom of God, as well as the responses from different kinds of people when they hear the Good News. The second kind of person Jesus describes proves the most instructive regarding the importance of Christian adolescents standing up to bullying when they experience or witness it. Jesus said that there is a certain kind of person (whom I call "Second Seed People") who initially receives the Good News about the kingdom of God with jubilation. They are the ones who are of "rocky ground" because "when trouble or persecution comes because of the word, immediately they fall away" (Mark 4:16–17). He said "they have no root in themselves and they do not endure" (Mark 4:17). Notice what Jesus did not say—that they had no rootedness within him. Rootedness and endurance are synonymous with perseverance, fortitude, and strength, all attributes of courage. The Hebrew word for courage, *hazaq*, means literally "to show oneself strong." Jesus tells us that there are people who were once excited about the Good News, but they don't have the guts to stay in the faith. They succumb to the corrosive influence of the sin of cowardice (Rev. 21:8).

Contrast this with those upon whom he heaped abundant praise: peacemakers who will be called children of God (Matt. 5:9).

When most Christians think of peacemaking, they think of the gentle and nice variety. Yet the word *peacemakers* here, unlike other portions of Scripture, does not imply passive nonresistance. It does not refer to those who do not fight, but to those who seek to bring solutions to conflicts.

Theologian David Hill notes that the word *peacemakers* was rarely used at that time. It most commonly referred to Roman Emperors who had brought peace.[3] Following this logic, Augustine suggested that peacemaking might include just war if the ruler could justify that war brought about greater peace. Of course, I'm not arguing for a physical war against bullying. But as you will see in the following pages, I do argue for a more muscular approach that finds its genesis within the spirit of what Jesus said, which requires more the spirit of a police officer than a nursery room volunteer.

More times than not, because of our misguided Niceness Doctrine, we think the gentle route is the only Christian route, leading to untold miscarriages of justice. Pastor Rick Warren notes:

> Peacemaking is not *avoiding conflict*. Running from a problem, pretending it doesn't exist, or being afraid to talk about it is actually cowardice. Jesus, the Prince of Peace, was never afraid of conflict. . . . Peacemaking is also not *appeasement*. Always giving in, acting like a doormat, and allowing others to always run over you is not what Jesus had in mind.[4]

The peacemaking Jesus talked about in the Beatitudes is not merely political or economic as in the Greco-Roman world, but peace that is also tethered to the Old Testament concept of *shalom*, "an inclusive expression of wholeness and well-being."[5] Peacemakers, therefore, are not simply those who bring peace between two conflicting parties, but those who actively work at making peace, bringing about wholeness and well-being *among the alienated*. Targets of serial bullying are among this beleaguered group.

When we consider the people who have made nations weep with appreciation and admiration, it's almost always people who were peacemakers: Abraham Lincoln, Sojourner Truth, Harriet Tubman, Dietrich Bonhoeffer, Mother Teresa, John Wesley, Mahatma Gandhi, Sophie Scholl, Dorothy Day, Desmund Tutu, Pope John Paul II, Gary Haugen, Swami Vivekananda, William Wilberforce, or my personal favorite, Martin Luther King Jr. A fire burned within them, and they were fueled by the knowledge that all people are imbued by their creator with honor, dignity, and immeasurable worth, which no person has the right to tear asunder.

That fire has yet to burn within contemporary Christianity when it comes to adolescent bullying. Bullying is the most prevalent form of injustice in our lives today, and it crosses all the usual barriers that divide us. No child, regardless of distinction, is immune or spared.

When we decide to participate in this holy battle, we will experience the joy of partaking in the work and will of God, and we will become different people as well. We will mature and be compassionate *and* courageous, kind *and* bold, tender *and* tough.

Right now, the lack of spiritual courage, which Jesus described in the Parable of the Sower, and the sin of cowardice are underreported reasons why Christian adolescents leave the faith—some never to return. Compounding this problem is a related reason why some 59 percent of millennials raised in the church have dropped out: few or none of these churches care about justice, especially for the least of these.[6] Millennials want a more biblical We-Church that includes spreading justice to all, not just an Us-Church that only meets the needs and desires of those within its walls.

Lack of spiritual courage is tearing our children from our faith and families. It also undercuts their relationships, their ability to overcome the crippling influence of fear and selfishness, their capacity to sustain a profitable career, their ability to defend their families and their nation, their confidence in standing against evil, and it makes them more susceptible to predatory crime and abusive bosses, spouses, spiritual leaders, and more since the quality of people's lives expands or contracts based upon the courage they possess or don't possess. Working for a bully, especially if you're female, can destroy a person's immune system, pushing women in particular to over-medicate and making them far more likely to consider suicide because they suffer the same effects of post-traumatic stress disorder (PTSD) as that of soldiers returning from war (some experts argue dropping the D since it's not a disorder but an injury). One of the greatest gifts we can give our children is spiritual courage, which "brings with it a great reward" (Heb. 10:35 GNT) and the ability to recognize and repel a life-stealing bully.

Security Blankets

Justice-free Christianity is a comfortable blanket that keeps us insulated from the harsher realities of life, which can be one reason why we go to church. The Barna Group survey in 2012 asked Christian women about the most important aspect of their life. This was no small question because not only do women make up the majority of people who attend church in America, they usually decide where a family goes to church. Women, especially married women, who continue to be the backbone of church attendees, said the well-being of their family is the top priority in their lives (53 percent) compared to their faith (just 16 percent).[7]

When family trumps all else, including faith, whatever is deemed safe and provides certainty is called "good," and whatever threatens safety and certainty is considered "bad." More so,

whatever is deemed nice is "Christian," and whatever and whom-
ever threatens niceness is deemed "unchristian." If we want to be
truly Christian, and if we want to rear children with deep strength
and character, we must be aware of this trap because comfort kills
spiritual growth.

But most of us who go to church were born into this safety-
first dynamic, a tenant of the Niceness Doctrine, so escaping it
won't be easy. And escaping it will make you appear odd, at least
at first. But staying in the comfort trap where we only care about
ourselves and our own makes us small-minded and small-souled.
God forbids us idols and safety-first security blankets because they
keep us from him. They aren't secure either. They're dangerous,
leading to spiritual veal and brittle spiritual bones. We become
unable to endure much, as the Parable of the Sower describes.

We must regain our justice-minded and prophetic spirit in the
church during these trying times within our nation for another
reason. Our star is fading. Fewer and fewer people attend and
believe. Laboring on behalf of justice is one of the few mediums
we have left to regain the world's trust and respect. If we don't, we
risk becoming a kind of irrelevant country club with tax-exempt
status. Many believe we already have.

Steps toward Courage

Parents and guardians, there are three steps you can expect your
child to take when they witness bullying: (1) intervene through
assertive but nonviolent words and behavior, (2) comfort the
target afterward, and (3) report (not tattle) to authority what they
witnessed. Any child can do one of the three. But it will take courage. When they do, they will become bigger, stronger people.

Adults, you have three opportunities before you as well. You
can share your time, treasure, or talent with a justice ministry. Join
one that speaks to your passions. You will help change personal

histories within the larger arc of history. You will mature in your faith as well, and your children will witness your commitment to what God loves.

But this courage I've described as so important to our children can take other forms as well. During one presentation in California where we provided a safe place to walk away from bullying, I watched a fourth grader stand up, walk across the gym, and apologize to another student. His classmates erupted in applause. This student began a domino effect in his school where more than fifty students apologized to one another in a span of about ten minutes.

Afterward, I talked to the boy who began this flood of righteousness. I asked him whom he had apologized to. He said his younger brother, Justice. He told me how happy he was to get that off his chest and that his act of courage encouraged others to apologize for bullying and related behaviors.

That can be you. That can be your child. But it won't come naturally. We must show and expect our children to love mercy, to be humble, and to act justly.

Notes

[1] Howard A. Snyder, *Liberating the Church: The Ecology of Church and Kingdom* (Eugene, OR: Wipf and Stock Publishers, 1996), 11.

[2] Martin Luther King Jr., "But, If Not," sermon delivered at Ebenezer Baptist Church in Atlanta, Georgia, November 1967, https://archive.org/details/MlkButIfNot.

[3] David Hill, *The Gospel of Matthew*, New Bible Commentary (Grand Rapids: Eerdmans, 1972).

[4] Rick Warren, *The Purpose Driven Life* (Grand Rapids: Zondervan, 2002), 153.

[5] Robert A. Guelich, *Sermon on the Mount: A Foundation for Understanding* (Waco, TX: Word, 1982), 91.

[6] Sam Eaton, "59 Percent of Millennials Raised in a Church Have Dropped Out—And They're Trying to Tell Us Why," Faithit.com, April 4, 2018, http://faithit.com/12-reasons-millennials-over-church-sam-eaton/.

[7]"Christian Women Today, Part 2 of 4: A Look at Women's Lifestyles, Priorities and Time Commitments," Barna Group 2012 Survey, August 16, 2012, https://www.barna.com/research/christian-women-today-part-2-of-4-a-look-at-womens-lifestyles-priorities-and-time-commitments/.

"Thank You for the Chance to Start Over"

At the conclusion of our *Courage to be Kind* assembly to fourth through eighth graders at Foothill Christian School in Glendora, California, we gave students the opportunity to give one another Vitamin A: a public apology for bullying and related behaviors.

The first apology, as usual, took the longest, and then the gym exploded with apologies. Soon, more than forty students not only apologized for bullying; they also apologized for moments of unkindness and meanness. One student apologized to his teacher for when he was unkind to her.

Students stood up and walked across the gym to offer sincere apologies. Their classmates cheered. Some cried. One student took my microphone near the stage and apologized to his classmate all the way in the back of the gym. He wanted to make sure that every student heard him so he would be held accountable. That's smart, because bullying is a temptation that revisits us. Like forgiveness, giving up bullying is almost always a process.

But it was the act of one girl that I remember most. She stood up, and with uncommon eloquence for her age, apologized to her entire class for bullying. She promised not to do it anymore. Then after the presentation, this fifth grader thanked me for calling her out, which was remarkable. Then she told me something even more memorable: "Thank you for giving me a chance to start over."

I could tell from her eyes and demeanor that she was a bright bully, a girl who could control her classmates with one word, even one look. I congratulated her for her courageous and humble act and warned her that the temptation to bully would likely return. Then I told her how I've noticed that many bullies are charismatic and have discernible leadership skills. But they lead others in the wrong direction.

"I can tell you're bright and people listen to you," I said. "Have you thought about leading them in a better way? Like supporting them instead? They'll follow you."

It was a new concept for her, but I could tell it was a penetrating one because the wheels behind her light blue eyes were spinning. "Your school is creating an anti-bullying group. You should join it," I said.

What makes the human heart listen to what is best within us? On this day, for this one girl, she told me. "What I liked about your message is that you said that this was a great day for kids who bully. It's a new day." She told me that she wanted an opportunity to start over but felt captive to her past and locked into the role of the class bully. Together with her school, we created a safe place to change, and the inspiration to take this unusual opportunity.

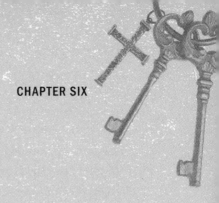

CHAPTER SIX

I Worship Me

Too many students, parents, and educators are still seduced by the easy promises of self-esteem.
—Dr. Roy Baumeister

Research has shown that people with overt low self-esteem aren't violent, so why would low self-esteem cause violence only when it is hidden? If you follow his train of thinking, you could come up with the sort of silly conclusion that covert low self-esteem causes aggression, but overt low self-esteem does not, which means concealment, not cockiness, is the real culprit. That makes little sense.
—Dr. Lauren Slater

WHEN SIGMUND FREUD ARRIVED IN ENGLAND AS AN AUSTRIAN REFUGEE IN 1938, LATE IN HIS LIFE, HE WAS immediately made a Fellow of the Royal Society, the highest scientific honor England could bestow. However, his contemporaries, like W. H. Auden, called him a "climate of opinion" and did not agree with all of Freud's largely unproven ideas.[1] In *Why Freud Was Wrong: Sin, Science, and Psychoanalysis*, Robert Webster argues that psychoanalysis is "perhaps the most complex and successful" pseudo-science in history.[2] One bias that contributed to Freud's pseudo-science was his hatred for religion, and especially Christianity, which blinded him to deeper and more common human longings. His bias and bigotry toward religion went so deep that as late as 1938, not long before his death, he claimed that Europe's real enemy was not the Nazis but the Catholic church.

Today, Freud's curious theories remain widely popular though they are no longer taught as authoritative. The man himself has been discredited as well as a habitual liar, plagiarist, dangerous manipulator, and creator of falsified evidence to support now discredited theories—many of the characteristics of a serial bully. Yet his gloomy climate of opinions still influences our daily discussions, especially when it comes to apprehending troubled minds and primal and disturbing urges. He introduced or made popular many terms in our lexicon: the "unconscious" (or subconscious), "Oedipus complex," "ego," "Freudian slip," "neurosis," "sibling rivalry," "libido," "psychosis," and "repression," among other terms.

Freud's writing is persuasive, penetrating, and admirably economical. His arguments can envelope the mind and quicken and haunt the imagination, as if you're discovering new psychological galaxies. He makes even the unthinking think, even if what they think is false.

We have been fooled by another pseudo-scientific discovery, and when it comes to bullying, there is none greater and more damaging: the Self-Esteem Movement, which also possesses quasi-religious qualities that include supposed deep wisdom and insight handed down from a founder or founders, texts and principles considered sacred, and a belief in things unseen but real. It too was ushered in with great fanfare but little scrutiny, creating a domino effect that we battle today. Like psychoanalysis, it was given the keys to each city across the land without vetting, starting with the urban, but now into every rural enclave as well. It was advertised as the wonder cure that would fundamentally transform human nature, raise test scores, and decrease domestic abuse and other forms of abuse and criminality, including bullying. It was supposed to make for a more civil, just, and loving society.

Origins

The Self-Esteem Movement is the problem child of the Positive Thinking Movement, which became popular after the Great Depression and World War II. Our world was ready for a more upbeat view of life after the horrors of war and economic devastation. Prior to that time, moral realists, who believed in distrust of the self and trusted institutions and customs outside the self to keep the self and society in check (the church comprised a large portion of moral realism then) had the upper hand against its opposing worldview: romanticism. "The realists believed in cultivation, civilization, and artifice; the romanticists believed in nature, the individual, and sincerity."[3]

Realism collapsed, not during the 1960s and 1970s as commonly thought, but during the 1940s and 1950s, the time of the Greatest Generation.[4] Our moral vocabulary shifted away from distrust in the human heart toward devotion to what it told us to do. Of course, it didn't happen overnight—it happened by degrees. Rabbi Joshua L. Liebman's 1946 *Peace of Mind* "urged people to engrave a new morality on their hearts, one based on setting aside the idea that you should repress any part of yourself." Instead, people should "love thyself properly . . . thou shalt not be afraid of thy hidden impulses . . . respect thyself . . . trust thyself."[5] It remained on the top of the *New York Times* best-seller list for an astounding fifty-eight weeks.

Other popular books continued to dismantle moral realism for a more feel-good approach to being human, culminating in the 1952 release of Norman Vincent Peale's mighty *The Power of Positive Thinking,* which remained the best-selling book for ninety-eight weeks. Humanistic psychology completed the assault on moral realism, led by Carl Rogers—one of the most influential psychologists of the twentieth century—who shifted us away from both Freud's brooding climate of opinion about human nature, as well as the historic Christian view of human nature. He and others argued that our largest psychological ailment is that we don't love ourselves enough, and a massive wave of self-love crashed across much of the developed world through therapists who took their cues from Rogers.

The new age of self-esteem was born.

The self-esteem craze made headlines in 1986 with the California Force to Promote Self-Esteem and Personal and Social Responsibility, a panel created by the California Legislature to conduct a three-year study on the topic with the hope that it would decrease anti-social behavior, including bullying. Yet as early as the 1970s, anti-bullying pioneer Dan Olweus, a research professor of psychology from Norway and the patriarch of today's anti-bullying movement, observed that children who bully do not exhibit behaviors common to low self-esteem, such as passivity, submissiveness, and risk-aversion. He observed that children who bully appear to enjoy harming and tormenting classmates.

One of the movement's earliest and most enthusiastic disciples was Dr. Roy Baumeister. "We had a great deal of optimism that high self-esteem would cause all sorts of positive consequences, and that if we raised self-esteem people would do better in life," he told the *New York Times.* "Mostly, the data have not borne that out."[6]

Initial data was promising but fleeting. Then came the crush of opposing research. In an extensive review of studies, Dr. Nicholas Emler, a social psychologist at the London School of Economics, found no clear link between low self-esteem and delinquency, violence against others, teenage smoking, drug use, or racism, though a poor self-image was one of several factors contributing to self-destructive behaviors like suicide, eating disorders, and teenage pregnancy.[7] High self-esteem, on the other hand, was positively correlated with racist attitudes, drunken driving, and other risky behaviors, including bullying. Though academic success or failure had some effect on self-esteem, students with high self-esteem were likely to explain away their failures with excuses, while those with low self-esteem discounted their successes as flukes. People with high self-esteem test higher on the happiness scale than those with lower self-esteem. They also take more initiative. But there is no correspondence to good or pro-social behavior.

As we did with Freud's psychoanalysis, we have spent so much time and energy dogmatically following the tenants of the Self-Esteem Movement that we've been pulled away from a more time-tested understanding of what it takes to be a successful, decent, and good person. "My bottom line," says Baumeister, "is that self-esteem isn't really worth the effort. Self-control is much more powerful."[8] Baumeister deepens his criticism:

> On the whole, benefits of high self-esteem accrue to the self while its costs are borne by others, who must deal with side effects like arrogance and conceit. At worst, self-esteem becomes narcissism, the self-absorbed conviction of personal superiority. Narcissists are legends in their own mind and addicted to their grandiose images. They have a deep craving to be admired by other people (but don't feel a special need to be liked—it's adulation they require). They expect to be treated as special beings and will turn nasty when criticized. . . . By most measures in psychological studies, narcissism has increased

sharply in recent decades, especially among young Americans.[9]

There is, however, one notable exception to the trend toward narcissism observed in psychological studies of young Americans, he says.

> It doesn't appear among young Asian-Americans, probably because their parents have been influenced less by the self-esteem movement than by a cultural tradition of instilling discipline. Some Asian cultures put considerably more emphasis on promoting self-control, and from earlier ages, than is common in America and other Western societies.[10]

He concludes: "Playground bullies regard themselves as superior to other children; low self-esteem is found among victims of bullies but not among bullies themselves. . . . Conceited, self-important individuals turn nasty toward those who puncture their bubbles of self-love."[11]

How Bullying and Social Science Are Killing the Self-Esteem Religion

Narcissism hit a new low when twenty-one-year-old Kimberley Davis hit a cyclist while driving and texting. Court records show she used her cellphone forty-four times around the time of the accident. She pulled over and did the legal thing and called for help. But she did the immoral thing and parked more than three hundred feet away from the victim who had a broken back, refusing to give him any aid. He spent the next three months in the hospital, unsure if he would walk again.

Davis told officers two days later: "I just don't care because I've already been through a lot of [$#&*] and my car is, like, pretty expensive and now I have to fix it. . . . I'm kind of [angry] that the cyclist has hit the side of my car." Davis, who studied beauty therapy, was indignant, taking to Facebook: "Never speed and do bad things so you lose your license kiddies! This sucks."

No remorse, no worries—other than to her precious car and freedom. To Davis and too many others, every day seems to be a Selfie Day. We agree that dangerous, self-centered, and arrogant Davis is broken like the cyclist's back. But what we have failed to see is that for more than fifty years, we've helped create such monsters among us through a belief as sacred to our secular culture as the Trinity is to Christians.

The Fallout

Unfortunately for today's youth, when we ask what self-esteem means to them, they usually answer with an example that is external, such as good grades, good looks, and an appearance of wealth. These externally driven students are more likely to suffer more problems, shows one study, when they enter their freshmen year in college. But students whose self-esteem is found within, such as possessing virtue or religious faith, fare better. "They are less likely to show anger and aggression and more restrained in their use of alcohol and drugs."[12]

The external markers for self-esteem put our children on very thin ice when circumstances change. They also lead to pride, arrogance, and self-absorption. The neutral, judgment-free language of psychology has finally beaten our common language and understanding of morality, confirming our worst fears of a declining morality, which I hear about when working with Christian and non-Christian schools. Before I spoke at a Christian education conference in Oklahoma, the president of the conference read from a conference flyer from twelve years previous. The topics discussed at that earlier conference were adherence to dress codes, curbing talking in the classroom, and the scourge of chewing bubble gum in class. The year I spoke, my topic was bullying—other topics included how to spot inappropriate sexual activity between students and teachers, and how to avoid student violence, including bringing weapons to school.

The excuse of low self-esteem has been used to explain away almost every human shortcoming, including intentional and sustained torment of others. It has thrown tremendous cover to schoolyard bullies for decades, enabling even more sustained campaigns of cruelty toward other children, like Alex Moore. While working with a public school in Texas, a school counselor told me that she was perplexed by the behavior of one of her school's "high flyers," a term she and others use to describe the cream of the crop. This exceptional student was the Student Body President and the standout on the debate team, yet she was also a tremendous bully. "I have to figure out how to help her grow her self-esteem," she told me, and asked me for advice. I explained to her that people with low self-esteem would never even run for Student Body President, and that they would probably never even ask to be on the debate team either. Both are high-profile behaviors, and people with low self-esteem avoid such exposure. They would feel like they were going off to a firing squad. I explained that this "high flyer" probably suffered from old-fashioned narcissism and predatory entitlement and needed an infusion of humility. I had gone against the quasi-religion of self-esteem and positive thinking, and it was not received well.

Yet remarkably, I have been admonished to not even use the word *bullying* to describe a bully, because such a label is damaging to the "self-esteem of a bully." Some have gone as far to say that the label itself is a form of bullying. After speaking to a crowded gym of high schoolers a few months before the 2016 general election,

I was approached by two young women who admonished me for being so "critical" of bullies. My criticism consisted of repeating what the experts tell us: that bullies are high on themselves. These young women were convinced that I had harmed the psyche of their classmates who needed "more love, not criticism." Then they repeated what is sacred text within the Self-Esteem Movement: "If you don't have anything nice to say, don't say anything at all."

I wasn't sure, but I was willing to bet that they weren't exactly fans of the Republican nominee for president. So I asked them, "Does that mean you can't say anything that's not nice about Donald Trump?" Their seemingly loving, dove-like, and concerned demeanor gave way to blunt anger that raced across their faces and appeared to swell within them. But to their credit, they didn't lie. They said that Trump deserved all the criticism he was receiving and more. By the way they spoke, it was clear to me that they didn't like him. I pointed out to them the obvious: that the dogmatic tenant of don't-say-anything-that-isn't-nice within the Positive Thinking/Self-Esteem ideology doesn't hold water and never did.

Empathy, the ability to understand and share the feelings of others, is essential in diminishing bullying because it helps instill within bystanders the ability to put themselves in the shoes of the target and feel what they feel, spurring intervention and comfort. Yet our campaign to bring generations of children more self-esteem has not created more empathy and may have actually diminished empathy through self-esteem's unintended side effect of greater narcissism. "People have become less empathetic—or at least they display less empathy in how they describe themselves. A University of Michigan study found that today's college students score 40 percent lower than their predecessors in the 1970s in their ability to understand what another person is feeling."[13]

Returning the Stigma

There was a time when being called a bully was one of the worst things you could be called, right up there with being called a racist. But that has changed directly because of the false ideology of the Self-Esteem Movement and the never-ending fog of neutral moral language that accompanies it. Correcting the myth that bullies aren't bad but broken is important because we must return the stigma of bullying. We do this because this is what gets a bully's attention. As seen earlier, possessing greater character is not as important to your average bully as is adulation. They seek the approval of their peers, so disapproval is one of the few tools we have available in our anti-bullying toolbox. We return the stigma not to rub their noses in their antisocial behavior, but to help liberate them from themselves, and liberate their many targets.

Harvard's Medical School helps us deepen this needed stigma. In *Almost a Psychopath*, Donald Schouten and James Silver reveal the terrifying behavior of those who have some but not all of the characteristics of a full-blown psychopath. Sadly, these people who in medical terms have a "subclinical disorder or subsyndromal condition" bring with them the "almost effect," making them even harder to spot and repel than a full-blown psychopath.[14] Schouten and Silver write:

> It's critical to recognize that the distinction between a psychopath and an almost psychopath is based not on the types of behaviors and emotional limitations but rather on the frequency and intensity of the behaviors and emotional (or, more accurately, emotionless) reactions to others. Almost psychopaths, like true psychopaths, may engage in socially unacceptable and sometimes illegal conduct, and again like true psychopaths, they may be self-centered, egotistical, and

indifferent to the needs and emotions of others. *The only real difference is the degree to which they exhibit these traits compared with true psychopaths.*[15]

Such people are, like many bullies, also glib but charming, narcissistic, grandiose, see themselves as superior to others, and aren't bound by society's rules and customs. They're manipulative, comfortable with lying, blame others for their behaviors, and have shallow emotions. When they do talk about emotions, their talk lacks any real sense of feeling.[16] "Even when their lies are discovered, any words of remorse are just that—words. . . . They may engage in aggressive and inappropriate conduct, ranging from harassment and stalking behaviors to thefts to malicious gossip."[17] School counselors and principals will say the same about the serial bullies they've known.

An almost psychopath in my life who was also a bully took me years to identify. I would often get a feeling of disquietude and uneasiness around her, even after just twenty minutes of conversation. Looking back, it was her facial expressions that really gave her away. We can all fake a smile with our lips, thinking that we've pulled off our deception. But it is very difficult to make your eyes smile at the same time, which completes the appearance of genuine friendliness. It takes a lot of practice to train your eyes to turn up at the corners, to look happy and inviting when you really aren't. Most people, like the former bully in my life, can't do it. Her smile was a lie and a mask. It was as if her face had two hemispheres—the lower part that knew it is important to appear friendly and inviting in order to get what you want, and the upper hemisphere where her eyes didn't smile and instead held a prowling nature. She has a history of abuse throughout the community, is arrogant, and is a world-class gossiper. The "almost effect" is evident to those who have the courage see it. "If a person's life and character is defined by a series of self-serving decisions reflecting an uncaring attitude toward others, the person is likely an almost psychopath."[18]

The similarities between bullying and almost psychopathy go even deeper still. Studies that examined the prevalence of sub-clinical psychopathy in the student populations in the United States and Sweden showed rates that range from 5 to 15 percent.[19] This means that for every twenty students, up to three of them fall within the almost psychopath range. *This is roughly the same number of students who bully.*

How do they slip by without being noticed until they've done so much damage? Their charm, manipulation, ease with lying, and gaslighting are part of the answer. But the other part is found within you and me as well. We don't see the almost psychopath bully because we don't think like one.

William March, author of *The Bad Seed*, says:

> Good people are rarely suspicious; they cannot imagine
> others doing the things they themselves are incapable
> of doing; usually they accept the undramatic solution as
> the correct one, and let matters rest there. Then too, the
> normal are inclined to visualize the [psychopath] as one
> who's as monstrous in appearance as he is in mind, which
> is about as far from the truth as one could well get.[20]

And we also don't want to believe they are among us. Worse, the self-esteem myth has trained us not to believe they're bad at all. We're willing to accept a 1 percent anomaly regarding human wickedness and evil. But not 5 to 15 percent. Yet the overlapping statistics give us a real lay of the land when considering how to best handle serial bullies, even if we don't have the guts to acknowl-edge it.

The Quasi-Religion

The belief that people do bad things because they feel badly inside is pervasive, sustained, and dogmatic, even when we have decades of data that destroy this claim. In my experience from speaking across this country to tens of thousands of schoolteachers, administrators, and parents, liberals have been far more dogmatic about the benefits of self-esteem than conservatives. While speaking in a predominately liberal community on the West Coast, I presented to my adult audience data debunking the myth of low self-esteem and bullying. I was interrupted right away, which was unusual since most people wait till Q&A to ask questions. One man stood up and angrily demanded that I recant my statement. I wouldn't. He said that because of what I said, nothing else I said could be trusted. He stormed out of the presentation in righteous indignation that would match that of any small-minded fundamentalist.

Anger steamed behind the eyes of others who didn't leave, but who gave me chilly stares instead. I challenged a major tenant of secular belief and they came out swinging, even after witnessing supporting data.

What is surprising and concerning to me, though, is how Christians and Christian leaders have accepted this dangerous myth. Christians in the anti-bullying effort have parroted this belief, saying that serial bullies, low on self-love, will change when flooded with love, compassion, and appeals to the Golden Rule. They have completely accepted the myth that self-hate, not self-love, is the root of the problem; and in doing so, they make the problem worse for countless targets and bullies.

After speaking at Saddleback church in Southern California three times in one day, a mother sternly disagreed with me after I challenged the self-esteem myth. She didn't ask me to recant, but she told me that there could be no other explanation as to why kids bully one another. I told her there was, and it comes from a traditional Judeo-Christian view that the human heart is predisposed toward pride and arrogance. She and the Christian speakers who speak about bullying have far more in common with contemporary humanistic psychology than with orthodox Christianity.

The Reality of Low Self-Esteem

As a former target of serial bullying, I know the heavy-footed life of low self-esteem with all that exhausting and unnecessary worry, fatiguing fear, self-doubt, and feelings of inferiority. And I also know what it's like to get healthy self-esteem back. I'll take the self-esteem years any day. There are many who, like I did at one time, need an infusion of self-esteem. Many groups of people have received a message from our culture that they are inferior to the rest. I hope that the Self-Esteem Movement has helped these groups and more to raise their sights and aspirations. Self-esteem is a helpful medicine when given to the right patients. Your average bully, however, is not one of them.

One group of people who may have revealed the folly of the Self-Esteem Movement more than any other were the rare and righteous few who helped and hid Jews during the Holocaust. On average, they did not possess any more self-esteem than their peers, so feeling good about themselves did not compel them to righteousness. They told researchers that the parental expectation to do the right thing regardless of hard circumstances and the Parable of the Good Samaritan were their guiding principles. These are sadly old-fashioned principles today. As Thoreau observed, "Every generation laughs at the old fashions, but follows religiously the new.[21]

If we embark on honest self-reflection, we'll find within ourselves a mixture of the secular and the sacred, saintly and profane. We are both, and all points in between. We're what one theologian called "glorious ruins"—so much cosmic potential, possibilities of glory, and ruinous egos, appetites, and habits. Our glory can be seen in our capacity for change, and we're burdened by how little we change. Our potential is our glory and our ruin. We're hot messes that can still do great things once we can untangle ourselves from the hot messes we keep making. We spin a complicated, torn, and rainbow-colored web.

But as is common with false religions, the Self-Esteem Movement says we're not this complicated. It's simplistic and dangerously reductionist; and because of these traits, it can't be trusted to lead us to wisdom and life because though truth can be simple, it's never simplistic. One way to reveal its fatal flaws is to ask the questions, *How come no person claims that her good deeds are at variance with her "Real Me"? Why is only bad behavior shrouded in Freudian mystery and intrigue? How come we put so much stock in an unproven theory?* As Dr. Lauren Slater writes, "covert low self-esteem causes aggression, but overt low self-esteem does not, which means concealment, not cockiness, is the real culprit. That makes little sense." What makes more sense is that this self-serving, self-soothing, and self-congratulatory belief was never true in the first place. And besides, why humble yourself when exalting yourself makes you feel so alive? Look at what we adults have done. We have put the safety of targets, the most vulnerable children in our neighborhoods and in our nation, in the hands an unproven theory about the roots of child-on-child aggression.

Think for a moment about all those parents, almost always mothers, who tell news crews that deep down inside, her son is really a good person. Her son who just murdered someone's daughter; her son who has a rap sheet literally the length of his arm.

He's a good kid; he just needs to walk taller and think better about himself, she says, parroting what has become a cultural proverb. But wait, he already walks like he's the most important person on the street. He already mean-mugs others because he thinks he's more important than all the other suckers in the neighborhood. He already lies with impunity, even to the people he claims to love, including that mother who's talking to the news crew.

When her criminal son uses the word "trust," it's not what non-bullies mean. He trusts people whom he can control—like we trust people who tell us the truth even if it hurts, through thick and thin. To him, trust means people do what he tells them to do, or at least won't oppose him. When he tells his mother, "You don't understand," he's not asking her to reflect with him as he tries to explain. It's a "tactical maneuver," writes Stanton E. Samenow for *Psychology Today*, "that takes the focus off the offender and puts others on the defense."[22]

He fits a common profile among criminologists, but a profile that popular culture doesn't want to see. This bully criminal has been twisting the meaning of words for most of his life. Like other criminals who are almost always bullies, he wrestled control away from his parent or parents at a very young age. He started his sadistic treatment on innocent animals, and then graduated to specific humans who wouldn't or couldn't push back, like his baby sister. Because his parent or parents were also duped by the Self-Esteem Movement, they didn't tell him that he should feel guilty about what he was doing to his defenseless sister because they believed guilt could be such a negative emotion and would harm his delicate self-esteem.

Because he is so arrogant, he finds provocation where there is none. When someone drives by in a great ride, he interprets this as an attempt to put him down, an intentional act of disrespect toward him. Criminals like him call this "flossing"—rubbing wealth in others' faces, so the driver *deserves* to be beaten and robbed. In the arrogant mind of a bully criminal, *he started it*. Victimologists call this a crime of resentment. But resentment is a common feeling. Why don't all people who experience resentment rob others? Because though we feel this deep negative emotion, we don't believe we have the right to actually attack the other person. Bully criminals believe they are the ones who deserve the limelight, new suit, and sweet ride. They are special by birth, not merit; the world just doesn't know it yet.

He brings the warped mind of a bully into his school as well. When asked by his friends why he's bullying this one boy, he responds, "Did you see the way he looked at me?!" It's the fabrication of a petulant, small, arrogant, and dangerous mind with growing upper body strength. But there was no look from the quiet and shy boy who wouldn't mean-mug another kid to save his life. His simpleton friends can't see through his lies and barbed charisma, and so neither can many adults.

You expect a mother to defend her son so pitifully. But you don't expect the audience to believe an excuse that should have died more than forty years ago. But we do. We, especially if we've never been bit by evil, have been charmed into thinking that such a person is actually a good person with rubble atop his goodness. There is rubble, but self-hatred isn't found there any more than it's found among other groups of kids. Self-hatred and low self-esteem are the millstones this bully thug puts around *his target's neck*. Some targets will never slip clear of theses millstones either, like the sister of a pastor in Chattanooga, Tennessee. He told me with tears in his eyes after my presentation that she had been bullied throughout high school, yet remarkably managed to get good grades. The summer after she graduated from high school, she went upstairs in the family house and has rarely left in the more than twenty-five years since. Serial female targets are twenty-five times more likely to develop agoraphobia. Bullying can even alter a person's DNA, especially the region that governs mood regulation. No college, no real friends, and no real life for her. She believes in Jesus, and she also believes what her bullies told her: that she's worthless, stupid, ugly, and worse. People high on self-esteem told her this.

Americans, author Barbara Ehrenreich reminds us, "did not start out as positive thinkers—at least the promotion of unwarranted optimism and methods to achieve it." Instead, as found in the Declaration of Independence, "the founding fathers pledged to one another 'our lives, our fortunes, and our sacred honor.'" The founding fathers had no certainty of winning a war for independence from England, an uncertainty that could cost them their lives. "Just the act of signing the declaration made them all traitors to the crown, and treason was a crime punishable by execution," she writes. "Many of them did go on to lose their lives, loved ones, and fortunes in the war. The point is, they fought anyway. There is a vast difference between positive thinking and existential courage."[23]

All of his life, Freud recalled how, when he was around ten years old, an anti-Semitic bully knocked his father's cap off and into the mud, shouting, "Jew, get off the pavement!" Injustice in the form of anti-Semitism in a nation where 90 percent of the population registered as Catholic redirected Freud's view of Christianity away from the admiration and respect he had previously held under the teaching of one former Catholic priest to what we know about him today. Injustice motivated him to discredit and destroy what he called the "religious *Weltanschauung*." Religion was "the enemy" that made him feel "inferior and alien."[24]

I wonder what would have happened to one of the most influential modern minds if someone of genuine faith had stood up for both him and his father, both targets of sustained bullying, so Freud would not feel inferior or alien, like the woman at the well whom Jesus blessed. They may have stemmed one of the most aggressive and sustained assaults on religious belief in modern time.

Right now there are children who live in self-described Christian communities who are losing their faith in Jesus with each bullying attack. They also feel inferior and alien. They need someone to say a redemptive "no" on their behalf, to show genuine faith in action. And the great thing is that this person doesn't have to possess shining self-esteem, just like those who helped Jews avoid humiliation and slaughter at the hands of the Nazis. This person can be, as the Apostle Paul said, one with a sober estimation of who they are: not low and not high. Equal. They just need stronger Christian conviction, not a devotion to the debunked Self-Esteem Movement.

Notes

[1] W. H. Auden, "In Memory of Sigmund Freud," in *Another Time* (New York: Random House, 1940), 102.

[2] Richard Webster, *Why Freud Was Wrong: Sin, Science, and Psychoanalysis* (New York: Basic Books, 1996).

[3] David Brooks, *The Road to Character* (New York: Random House, 2015), iBooks.

[4] Brooks, *Road to Character*, iBooks.

[5] Brooks, *Road to Character*, iBooks.

[6] Erica Goode, "Deflating Self-esteem's Role in Society's Ills," *New York Times*, September 30, 2002.

[7] Goode, "Deflating Self-esteem's Role."

[8] Goode, "Deflating Self-esteem's Role."

[9] Roy F. Baumeister and John Tierney, *Willpower: Rediscovering the Greatest Human Strength* (New York: Penguin Group, 2011), iBooks.

[10] Baumeister and Tierney, *Willpower*.

[11] Roy F. Baumeister, "Violent Pride," *Scientific American* 17, no. 4 (August 2006): 99.

[12] Baumeister, "Violent Pride."

[13] Brooks, *Road to Character*, iBooks.

[14] Ronald Schouten and James Silver, *Almost a Psychopath: Do I (or Does Someone I Know) Have a Problem with* Empathy? (Center City, MN: Harvard Medical School, 2012), 9.

[15] Schouten and Silver, *Almost a Psychopath*, 47.

[16] Schouten and Silver, *Almost a Psychopath*, 47.

[17] Schouten and Silver, *Almost a Psychopath*, 48.

[18] Schouten and Silver, *Almost a Psychopath*, 49.

[19] Schouten and Silver, *Almost a Psychopath*, 57.

[20] Schouten and Silver, *Almost a Psychopath*, 57.

[21]Thoreau, Henry D., *Walden* (New York: Thomas Y. Crowell, 1910), 32.

[22]Stanton E. Samenow, "The Criminal's Use of Everyday Words," *Psychology Today*, June 5, 2017, https://www.psychologytoday.com/blog/inside-the -criminal-mind/201706/the-criminals-use-everyday-words/.

[23]Barbara Ehrenreich, *Bright-Sided: How the Relentless Promotion of Positive Thinking Has Undermined America* (New York: Metropolitan Books, 2009), 14.

[24]Armand Nicholi, *Question of God: C. S. Lewis and Sigmund Freud Debate God, Love, Sex, and the Meaning of Life* (New York: Free Press, 2002), 21.

Healing Broken Hearts,
with Dr. John Townsend

Dr. John Townsend has written or cowritten thirty books, including the *New York Times* best-selling Boundaries series, a resource The Protectors recommends more than any other to targets of bullying, their parents, and their related guardians. He is a passionate child advocate and an active board member of Mustard Seed Ranch, a residential program for abused children.

Q: John, targets of serial bullying are often kind, gentle, shy, and even meek. They're often really nice kids. How do you help such people see that self-defense, saying no, and standing up for themselves and others is not inherently unchristian?

I see this quite a bit. I take them to the Bible to show them that it doesn't say standing up for yourself is wrong. We are supposed to take a stand. When Dr. Henry Cloud and I wrote *Boundaries*, we found more than three hundred Scriptures that encourage us to create strong boundaries in our lives. For example, in Proverbs 4:23, we're told, "Above all else, guard your heart, for everything you do flows from it" [NIV]. "To guard" in Hebrew means to keep watch over your inner person, your passions, feelings, thoughts, decisions, and values. We're supposed to guard them because they can be affected and taken away. The Bible says we should do this "above all else," so it's of the highest priority. It is from the heart that the issues of life flow—everything we do and contribute to the world comes from our hearts. So if we don't set boundaries, we will be ineffective regarding God's mission for our lives. Setting boundaries, far from being selfish, is really good stewardship of our lives.

Q: What are your thoughts about telling a child to "turn the other cheek" when he experiences bullying?

Anytime we take one passage out of context and we don't balance it out with what the Bible says about similar matters, we can get into trouble really quickly. If we're not careful, we'll end up on an island drinking Kool-Aid. We must have balance. We also must remember that not every Scripture applies to children. It's written to adults. I would never advise a parent to tell their child to accept bullying because it's not good for the child, and it's not good for the bully because it may help the bully become even more narcissistic.

Q: As a psychologist, what have you seen as the result of ongoing bullying to children?

What I have seen in my clinical practice with bullied children is damage to their character. Our character is a set of capacities required to meet the demands of reality. It includes how we handle our faith, workout, make money, pay bills, take care of our families, keep our integrity, and more. Without these skills in our toolbox, we suffer all kinds of problems, including addictions and relational problems.

Bullying harms a person's ability to trust others and feel vulnerable in a safe way. It makes it hard for them to be separate, independent people and to have their own voice. They have a harder time dealing with negative realities and believe that they are always at fault and judge themselves unfairly. As adults, they often become codependent, and it's harder for them to find their mission and purpose, discover their talents and passions, and then make a difference in this world.

Q: Targets of bullying sometimes fall on the more passive side of life. How do you help a more passive person become an assertive person?

Passive people can get stuck in the three Ps of learned helplessness: all their struggles are personal, pervasive, and permanent. They learn how to give up on things instead of making their dent in the world.

The best way to help them is for them to have people who believe in them and support them, people who are empathetic and deeply in tune with them. They need to know that they aren't alone with their fears. Help them assert themselves in small increments so they can stretch themselves. For example, we can hold them accountable to help them speak their mind. Give them the freedom to disagree with you and at the same time be supportive and embrace them.

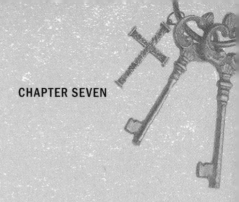

CHAPTER SEVEN

Prey for Me

Humility is the great omission and failure in my eleven years of preaching. I believe that this is my greatest oversight both in my example and in my instruction. I therefore do not claim to be humble. I do not claim to have been humble. I am convicted of my pride.[1]
—Mark Driscoll

DISGRACED PASTOR MARK DRISCOLL OF SEATTLE, WASHINGTON, WHO IMPLODED MARS HILL CHURCH ISN'T THE first megachurch pastor to be accused of bullying, and he won't be the last. Darrin Patrick, lead pastor of The Journey, a St. Louis, Missouri, megachurch, was also dismissed for heavy handed and unrepentant leadership tactics. Patrick was the vice president of Acts 29, a church-planting network. Driscoll was its cofounder, raising very serious concerns as to whether or not others within that network have the same deficiency of character.

Jimmy Dodd, president of PastorServe (a ministry that provides crisis and preventative assistance to pastors and their churches) initially worked with Patrick as part of his restorative process. He says that the Driscoll debacle helped the church finally name an ongoing problem. "There was a belief among church leaders," he says, "that you could fire a guy for moral failure, and lack of financial integrity, but couldn't fire a pastor for being a bully. Driscoll changed that." Dodd says that because of the high-profile fiascos like Driscoll and Patrick, more and more churches are seeing bullying as a fireable offense. These firings, says Dodd, have given church leaders across the country the confidence and courage to do the right thing. "The elders at Darrin's church took courage from what they saw happen at Seattle."[2]

Driscoll, Patrick, and other high-profile pastors who did not make the national news for bullying but who were still removed due to abusive behavior help us pull back the covers on how toxic bullies really think and feel about themselves and others. They also show us that no place is free from the bullying personality, especially since bullies have discernible gifts that make them valuable to an organization. In fact, the places bullies can do the most damage to an organization are vocations that attract more nurturing personalities, such as nursing, teaching, and ministry. This is because bullies know how to steamroll. The nurturing personality can be conflict averse, so when they witness bullying inside or outside of church, they are prone to hide, pretend it's not happening, and give it another name. Because they follow the discredited "Wounded Bully" theory—supposing bullies have crippling insecurities and unrecognized shame—the nurturing personality will try to nurture such a person back to life, admonishing themselves to heap more love, concern, and tender care upon the bully. By now, you can see that this is often a disastrous response when applied to serial bullies.

Nurturing people are kind, peaceable, and trusting. They may have been wounded, some deeply. The comfort church provides them is very attractive and sometimes blinds them to the real behaviors of others. And because they don't bully, they can't and won't believe that people who claim to speak for God would deliberately and serially harm others to get what they want. Since they don't kiss up to some people and kick down others the way bullies do, they can't fathom that other people can be so deliberately duplicitous. So they seek answers and resolutions that actually go against what the Bible says. Their personality makes them especially vulnerable to bullies, and gullible in their acceptance of dishonest excuses, dissimulation, and subterfuge. They are kind but not always wise. Blinded by unwarranted optimism in human nature, they want to believe the best in other people, even when they are standing before someone who regularly destroys others to feed their ego, appetites, and ambition.

To be clear, pastors who want to see their vision of ministry actualized and expect others to perform their duties, business leaders who drive a hard bargain, teachers who are demanding, bosses who expect projects to be done on time and well, and hard-nosed coaches are not automatically bullies. Getting our feelings hurt by a boss, teacher, coach, or pastor doesn't mean we were bullied, either. In fact, tough leadership often exposes the true character of others and then helps them grow and improve. But, bullies are more than happy to masquerade as tough leaders—if that's what is needed to get them off the hook. Still, they remain a very different bird with veiled and dark plumage.

As a reminder, it's important to remember that there are roughly two groups of kids who bully. One group experiments with the pleasure of bullying the way a person might experiment with drugs, sex, and other risky behavior. But they don't become full-blown bullies. They don't do it enough to have bullying become part of their core behavior or identity. To put this in biblical terms, they don't succumb to wickedness. We call these students *acute bullies* who, when confronted with the reality of their behavior, change. Like many students, they're aware that what they're doing is wrong, even though it's so much fun, but they aren't fully aware of the impact of the bullying upon their target. They tend to be more thoughtless than malicious. When the reality of their bullying is revealed to them, they don't try to minimize their behavior. Instead, they will say, "I didn't know they [the target] were taking it so hard," and they aren't lying. They are inclined to apologize as well, though sometimes they need guidance and prodding since offering an apology requires humility and courage.

The following information doesn't apply to most cases of acute bullying.

What you're about to read describes the mindset and orientation of *serial bullies*, which represent the worst in human nature and behavior, requiring a kind of behavioral solvent that our culture has yet to create and apply.

Beyond Anger: Contempt and Disdain

Americans collectively gasped when Sheriff Grady Judd announced the arrest of two girls, aged twelve and fourteen, charged with aggravated stalking of twelve-year-old Rebecca Sedwick of Lakeland, Florida. Rebecca committed bullycide by jumping from a silo on September 9, 2013. "The malicious harassment by [the two suspects] was likely a contributing factor in Rebecca's decision to commit suicide," explained Judd. The sheriff's department said Rebecca was told through cyberbullying, "Drink bleach and die," "You should die," and "Why don't you go kill yourself?"

But that isn't what caused our nation to shudder, given how common such stories have become. What caused many to put a hand over their mouth in disbelief was what one of these juveniles did soon after Rebecca's death. The fourteen-year-old suspect wrote on Facebook, "Yes I know I bullied Rebecca and she killed herself and I don't give a [$#*!]." That brazen and audacious statement compelled Judd to arrest the two juveniles.

Bullies have attacked their prey and their prey's families even after their victims have committed bullycide by writing slanderous and disparaging comments online. After thirteen-year-old Rosalie Avila of Yucapcia, California, hanged herself due to more than two years of bullying, her parents were psychologically attacked and her memory was mocked when her parents received an image of Rosalie's face superimposed onto another person's body. She is shown giving a thumbs down next to a bed. The message next to it read, "Hey mom. Next time don't tuck me into this." Underneath was another image of their daughter's head superimposed onto a body with its arms and hands pointing toward a freshly dug grave. The message next to this horrifying image read, "Tuck me into THIS."

Instead of remorse, regret, or shame, some bullies and their troll supporters gloat over the harm they inflicted upon others, and they labor to destroy the vestige of their victims' memories. Some even record their abuse on their cellphones to show others and to publish their attacks on Facebook. They say they would do it again, and those of us who don't bully are mystified. We wouldn't be if we understood how serial bullies really think and feel.

Most serial bullies aren't motivated primarily by anger, or by an inability to control their anger. Bullies are motivated by something far worse: disdain and contempt.

The late Dr. Robert Solomon of the University of Texas in Austin was a pioneer in the study of these dangerous emotions that motivated many of history's despots and dictators—bullies of the highest order. Dr. Solomon explains that we express resentment toward those we perceive above us, anger toward those of equal status, and contempt and disdain toward those we perceive are below us.

Those consumed by contempt believe others (including institutions) are inferior and unworthy of respect (for instance, the way an arrogant criminal refuses to show the law and its officers the respect they deserve). Unlike anger, which is hot but short-lived, contempt and disdain are cooler but longer lasting, helping us to see why some bullies are so tenacious—even beyond the grave. Worse, many serial bullies believe the object of their contempt lacks value and may even be worthless. They lack compassion and empathy, not because they are incapable of expressing these emotions, but because they perceive themselves as above the herd. They make lists of "bad qualities" of others and harbor a "positive self-feeling" about themselves, thinking themselves superior. Bullies may even feel that others must be warned about the bad qualities of their targets. Some believe they are part of a moral campaign to marginalize their target for the good of others.

Countless atrocities are committed for similar reasons, including Hitler's countless murders due to his contempt for Jews, homosexuals, and those physically and mentally challenged. These people did nothing personal to Hitler or his racist henchmen, just as Sheriff Judd said he could find no evidence that Rebecca harmed her attackers. Their existence alone was worthy of scorn because they were viewed as subhuman, less than. Bullying expert Barbara Coloroso, in *Extraordinary Evil: A Short Walk to Genocide,* writes, "Once human beings feel the cold hate of contempt for other human beings, they can do anything to them and feel no compassion, guilt, or shame; in fact they often get pleasure from the targeted person's pain."[3]

I'm Special, So Special

As explained earlier, our world is at the tail end of a forty-year experiment that has gone against the grain of thousands of years of belief, and created a bold, intriguing, and seemingly humane hypothesis: bullies do bad things to others because they are really shame-encrusted people trying desperately to hide their shame from others, creating what psychologists call a "mask." So they try to alleviate their shame by impregnating other children with the seed of shame, making them also feel like losers. This unrecognized shame, we're told, behaves like a virus within a computer's operating system, causing the child to commit mistakes the way a computer virus corrupts the computer's operating system. This hidden shame, we've been told, is implanted during childhood, usually by family or related caregivers. An interview with Jennifer LaFleur greatly challenges this belief and helps us see even more clearly how bullies operate.

During her eye-opening interview with The Canadian Broadcast Company (CBC), this self-professed Canadian "mean girl" admits she was a selfish and self-centered child who came from a healthy home where she never experienced one day of abuse. Today, she helps targets escape bullying. But when she was in just fourth grade, she created an all-girls-club for the sole purpose of excluding and harming another girl who did nothing wrong to her. She drafted a contract that she demanded ten other girls in her class sign, swearing to "hate" this other girl. All ten signed it.

What made this cruel, arrogant, and abusive Queen Bee change her bullying ways? It was the wisdom of her high school art teacher who knew that what Jennifer really needed wasn't more self-esteem. She made Jennifer a peer advisor for a younger mean girl. Jennifer soon saw her own dominating behavior in the life of another person, which woke her up. She saw herself in another's selfish and cruel eyes, and saw the light.

But this wasn't the only ray of penetrating light that brought sobriety. Jennifer was bullied by Debbie, a much more powerful bully. Jennifer began to feel what her targets felt. And Debbie didn't stop. Of all the reasons we The Protectors hear as to what stops bullies, being bullied themselves is the leading reason.

LaFleur shatters the "all-bullies-have-low-self-esteem" myth when she admits, "I was selfish and self-centered, which stops you from having sympathy and empathy" for those who are outside your circle of concern.

Most kids, she says, are unwilling to admit they bully, even when confronted with a mountain of evidence. And she laments that one of the hardest parts of her job is to get their parents to admit it as well. She says bullies have high self-esteem derived from wrong values. They base their esteem on power and control, not merit or achievement. She says they need guidance using their power for good, helping them feel how good it is to help people instead of using that same power to harm them.[4]

In *The Narcissism Epidemic*, authors Jean M. Twenge and W. Keith Campbell remind us that, "Some schools that teach social skills and conflict resolution also teach 'I am special.' This is a bad idea—the two can potentially cancel each other out." Instead, they say, we should be vigilant against the narcissism that helps create children who bully. "Narcissistic kids fight when insulted, not the low self-esteem kids (who are likely to do nothing). Teaching kids how special they are makes things worse, not better. . . . By most measures in psychological studies, narcissism has increased sharply in recent decades, especially among young Americans."[5]

When surveyed, 39 percent of American eighth-graders were confident in their math skills. Korean students the same age were only 6 percent confident. The Korean students, however, far exceeded the American students' "actual performance on math tests."[6] American kids are number one in thinking they're number one.

We know that their behavior is harmful to others as well as to themselves—but do bullying children exhibit some degree of psychopathy?

According to the American Psychiatric Association, antisocial personality disorder (the closest diagnosis the *DSM–IV–TR* has to psychopathy), like all personality disorders, "cannot be officially diagnosed before the age of eighteen, although mental health experts can identify psychopathic traits before that time."[7] This manual points out that personality disorders begin by late adolescence or early adulthood. But the signs of adult personality disorders—including antisocial, borderline, and narcissistic—can be detected even in childhood. "Studies have shown that personality traits are present from the earliest days of infancy. It follows, then, that it should be possible to measure certain characteristics of psychopathy—shallow affect, lack of empathy, and so on—before a person reaches adulthood."[8]

Such people "target the vulnerable, steal from the unwary, and deceive the weak (or, even more to their delight, the strong) if they can get away with it."

While their ways can be violent and callous, their demeanor, say Schouten and Silver, is often the opposite, helping them make a very good first impression that lowers the guard of their targets. They have a "glibness and charm that enables them to manipulate others and sometimes achieve success and apparent normalcy in their work and personal lives." And like serial bullies, "Even when forced into treatment, psychopaths are likely to have only superficial and temporary motivation, lasting only as long as the treatment is mandated or until the psychopath can generate a reason to be excused."[9] School counselors tell me that they can rarely, if ever, get a serial bully to truly change how they mistreat others. "They usually throttle their behavior back just enough so they don't get expelled," said one counselor from a Christian school in Minnesota.

Both serial bullies and almost psychopaths engage in reactive and instrumental aggression, which is predatory and preplanned—also called "proactive aggression." Both types of people are dangerous, even while they show a pleasant demeanor. Schouten and Silver's goal, like mine, isn't to tar and feather such children, but to alleviate pain and suffering now, and prevent more serious problems later for the serial bully, her targets, and the moral consternation and fallout their bystanders will contend with, some for the rest of their lives.

Under My Thumb

The overlap with narcissistic personality disorder (NPD) is worth exploring as well. Such people lack the ability to empathize with others and have an inflated sense of self-importance. Traits include grandiosity, lack of empathy, and a need for admiration.

> People with this condition are frequently described as arrogant, self-centered, manipulative, and demanding. They may also concentrate on grandiose fantasies (e.g., their own success, beauty, brilliance) and may be convinced that they deserve special treatment. These characteristics typically begin in early adulthood and must be consistently evident in multiple contexts, such as at work and in relationships.[10]

Feigned Sorrow, False Friendships, and Empty Promises

A letter published by the church leaders at The Journey gives us insight into a common ploy of serial bullies: empty promises. Elders said they confronted Patrick for years about his behavior. "They were met, initially, with contrition on Patrick's part, but he 'quickly receded into unfulfilled promises, reversion of old patterns, and broken trust with pastors and elders.'" The letter from the elders also mentioned "deep sin patterns," including "refusal of personal accountability, manipulation and lying, misuse of power/

authority, [and] a history of building his identity through ministry and media platforms."[11]

Feigned sorrow and empty promises tear at the fabric of our relationships. But it's false friendships that cut the deepest. After one presentation to more than 1,200 high schoolers, a distraught and dazed junior walked up to me and needed a hug. She had been crying and looked like she had seen a ghost.

"When you talked about bullies pretending to be friendly, you just described my best friend," she said, crying again. She was staggering mentally, trying as best she could to reconcile the insight she was given with her experiences with her "best friend" for the last two years. The person she thought was her BF was in reality her greatest bully.

False friendships are among the most shattering revelations when it comes to bullying, and a revelation I don't present lightly, because it comes from the deepest parts of infidelity and betrayal. It is one thing for an enemy to abuse you, but a *"friend"*? It's an overwhelming truth, even for adults.

Such an ability to deeply deceive goes against another prevalent myth: bullies are powerful but oafish thugs with little, if any, understanding about social dynamics. These deeply insecure and anxious children heavy step their way through life, making them easy to spot and sequester. In reality, according to Jon Sutton, Peter Smith, and John Swettenham from the Department of Psychology at Goldsmiths College, London, there is a "general lack of support for this notion." Instead, they note:

> These bullies, being cold, manipulative masters of a social situation, may be resistant to traditional anti-bullying policies and curriculum work, and require new and innovative techniques. In the worst scenario, intervention

strategies emphasizing understanding of others may be inadvertently honing the skills of such a bully.[12]

Bullies are often charming and friendly—as long as you keep giving them what they want. But like other aspects of their lives, they're posing, pretending, and playing others. There are many common signs of an unhealthy friendship, such as only having time for you when it benefits them, putting you down in front of others, and breaking important promises. Bullying goes beyond bad friendships that can stem from thoughtlessness and immaturity. Their harmful behaviors are intentional and premeditated. For example, they deliberately exclude you when they can (as opposed to just forgetting) and withhold information from you that would be beneficial to you. But here's the one harmful behavior they commit that can help you see your bully for who she really is. *Bullies don't celebrate your successes.* They often belittle and discount them. Remember that in their arrogant mind, you and others are below them, so who are you to surpass them? It's undeserved. A fluke. A cruel hoax that the universe has created against them, so time to get you back into line, behind them.

But to expose your fake friendship for what it really is, sharing your victories and good news isn't enough. You have to surprise them—not to be cruel, but so you can get the best information possible. Because bullies are so calculating, they are very good at hiding how they really think and behave. To get past their ability to dissimulate, spring your good news on them and say it with excitement. Then watch how they *really* respond as opposed to how you think they should respond, or how you want them to respond.

If I had done this during a key time in my adult life, I would have saved myself and my family a mountain of emotional turmoil. I vividly remember sharing some great news with three couples who were friends of ours: due to the blood, sweat, and tears I endured as a coach, my children were able to go to the best private school in our region. Two of the couples responded as if we had killed their pet. They looked at us with anger in their eyes. One actually said to her browbeaten husband, "Let's go." They just walked away. The third couple responded with genuine glad tidings. They smiled and gave us a hug.

The two couples that behaved as if they had just received some of the worst information imaginable were the two worst bullies—male in one couple, female in the other—in our adult lives. We no longer have relationships with them—not because of this one event, but because of subsequent bullying and related behaviors. The one couple that celebrated our victory remains among our closest friends.

Each of the bullies had married someone who became their enabler, regularly making excuses for their bully spouse. I've noticed how the supposed "good" spouse became more like the bully spouse. Having observed marriages with one bullying spouse, I have yet to see the bully spouse become more like the better, non-bullying spouse. The darkness in the bully is more powerful and penetrating than the supposed goodness in the other spouse, causing me to conclude that the goodness within the better spouse wasn't really goodness at all. It was niceness, the disease to please others, even if that means making excuses for wicked behavior. Both of these couples attend church. One was a missionary.

When we announced that great news, unbeknownst to me, I was given the gift of objectivity, and I didn't receive it. Reality stared me in the face that day, yet it was so contrary to what I thought was the case that it went right over my head. Had I been more aware of the dynamic around me and courageous enough to see it, I would have saved myself so much pain and suffering later. So targets, surprise your "friend" with some great development in your life, then watch how they really respond. Don't sugar coat their response. You just might save yourself from a mountain of grief as well.

What Bullies Need: Humility

All bullies lack humility, which is another way of saying they're prideful and arrogant. So Driscoll's admission that his inability to be humble was one of the greatest problems within his ministry—a problem that eventually took him down—is a source of great shame, but also possible liberation and redemption.

Instead of promoting greater self-esteem, we as a culture should be promoting greater humility as an antidote to bullying, which is far more likely to lead to personal success and a healthier society. New research from Duke University suggests that people with higher intellectual humility are better at making meaningful decisions because they are better at discerning the quality of evidence. Lead author Mark Leary, professor of psychology and neuroscience, says that people with high intellectual humility may have a greater ability to keep their "ego out of their intellectual decisions," and discern the difference between weak information and fact-backed information.[13] To put it another way, such people are wiser than those with low intellectual humility.

In his business classic *Good to Great*, Jim Collins reveals the characteristics of business leaders who take their good company to the next level. One of the characteristics that these leaders had in common was genuine humility. Top CEOs, contrary to popular myth, are modest and are free of blinding pride and hubris, helping them to treat others better and transform doubts into the creation of better products and services. These CEOs are "Level 5" leaders who are often not charismatic, ultra-confident people. They are humble, avoid the limelight, work diligently, and continually improve themselves.

Humility is a key to self-understanding and the accumulation of wisdom and compassion. It stretches us and aids new growth within ourselves—to the betterment of others. Instead of encouraging students to write love letters to and about themselves, schools across our country should be giving serial bullies what David Brooks calls a Humility Code instead. He lists fifteen points to this code in his book *The Road to Character*. It includes maxims such as, "We don't live for happiness, we live for holiness," and "We are all ultimately saved by grace." But points 3 and 4 are the ones that best apply as antidotes for bullying:

3. Although we are flawed creatures, we are also splendidly endowed. We are divided within ourselves, both fearfully and wonderfully made. We do sin, but we also have the capacity to recognize sin, to feel ashamed of sin, and to overcome sin. We are both weak and strong, bound and free, blind and far-seeing. We thus have the capacity to struggle with ourselves.

4. In the struggle against your own weakness, humility is the greatest virtue. Humility is having an accurate assessment of your own nature and your own place in the cosmos. Humility is awareness that you are an underdog in the struggle against your own weakness. Humility is an awareness that your individual talents alone are inadequate to the tasks that have been assigned to you. Humility reminds you that you are not the center of the universe, but you serve a larger order.[14]

If Alex Moore's tormentors had been given this script to contemplate, if they had been given a homework assignment on these two points alone, I believe some would have stopped their ongoing campaign of cruelty against her.

Parents—Praise Effort, Not (Supposed) Innate Ability

In *Mindset: The New Psychology of Success,* Dr. Carol Dweck popularized the idea of categorizing people as having either a fixed mindset or a growth mindset. This distinction remains very popular within education today and asserts that children with fixed mindsets believe that life revolves around absolutes that may or may not be within their control. The student with a fixed mindset falls roughly into two camps. One is the "Why Try" child who believes skills and aptitudes are fixed or endowed somehow, and they don't have them. The other camp, the "Big Me" child, believes skills and aptitudes are fixed—and they have mountains of both, even when they don't. They are exceptional because they live. They are fixed at the head of the pack, and woe to anyone who gets ahead of them. The Big Me child is prone to believe she's superior to others, so mistakes, failures, and setbacks are poisonous to them and must be discarded. Blaming their targets is a natural response, as is flat-out lying. They spend too much time comparing themselves to others instead of hunkering down and doing the hard things, like studying and self-reflecting. They don't aspire to be great. They believe they already are.

It doesn't come as a surprise that fixed-mindset children are more prone to damaging interpersonal relationships, says Dweck. For example, their ideal partner is someone who worships them by constantly validating and praising their fixed qualities, even when they don't exist. Compare this to a person who has a growth mindset who seeks relationships that spur their inner growth by challenging them. To a fixed-mind person, such challenge feels like an offense.

To raise growth-minded children who believe that intelligence can be developed and who are far less likely to bully, Dweck advises us not to associate good grades and other achievements with innate intelligence with statements such as "You're so smart at whatever you do." Rather, praise and highlight persistence and hard work. Praise for naturally endowed ability as opposed to earned ability is the main reason why children have a fixed mindset, which can lead to inordinate self-esteem that can lead to bullying.

Uniquely Human

The late Henri Nouwen was a former professor at Notre Dame, Yale, and Harvard who later worked at the L'Arche community of Daybreak in Richmond Hill, Ontario, with developmentally disabled persons.

His main topic during an intriguing lecture was the traits that make us uniquely human. He explained how anthropologists and evolutionary psychologists provided the following examples as proof of our uniqueness: self-awareness, symbolic cognition, and the capacity to imagine, among other traits. These, he noted, are all mind-centered, which academics and many others believe is the centerpiece of what distinguishes humans from other living beings.

Then he dropped a moral bombshell, and one we must contend with today: If the mind is the defining attribute that makes us human, what about those whose minds are diminished, like the eighteen-year-old mentally challenged man who in January 2017 was tortured by four individuals in Chicago who arrogantly broadcasted that torture live on Facebook? The disturbing thirty-minute video shows a man tied up and his mouth covered, cowering in the corner of a room. His attackers laugh arrogantly and shout with a perverse pleasure, "$#&*! Donald Trump" and "$#&*! white people" as they kick and punch him. The mentally challenged young man yells, "Why are you doin' this?!" We put on Facebook events that bolster our online persona and reputation. We record what we're proud of and keep on our phones what we value. To the Chicago four, that day was worth commemorating.

According to a prosecutor and court documents, those sadists forced him to drink toilet water, gagged him, and bound his hands. And while the young man can be heard screaming, one of the assailants walked up to him with a knife and asked if he should "shank" him. One of the male suspects used a knife to cut the man's sweatshirt and hair, exposing part of his bloodied scalp.

I've been held at knifepoint twice. It's horrific. The panic, terror, confusion, and dizziness assail your mind long after you're safe. So I'm grateful to see the success of a GoFundMe campaign for this young man. More than $100k was raised early on to help him and his family.

Mentally and physically challenged people are among the most bullied—possibly the *most* bullied group—in America and throughout the world. They are easier targets. Some are painfully naive about dissimulation, so they're unable to discern the way bullies feign friendship in order to gain their trust. But the main reason is more sinister. Many who bully don't believe that the mentally and physically challenged are fully human. Of course, they don't come out and say this when interviewed. They don't tattoo this belief on their foreheads or forearms. But they proclaim it loud and clear through their behaviors. Their arrogance compels them to believe that physically and mentally challenged people deserve disdain, contempt, and even torture.

As an expert witness, I help juries understand why bullies bully. I explain how they, like the Chicago Four, record their sinister acts because they are actually proud of them. I explain how they enjoy dominating and controlling others, especially the mentally and physically challenged. Like Trevor, who attended a private school in the Midwest, and who, due to cerebral palsy, walked with the help of leg braces and crutches.

Jurors heard how he was kind to his classmates, but his good character didn't matter to a group of kids who made his life a living hell. They encouraged him to kill himself, punched him repeatedly from behind, and pushed him to the ground more times than he could remember, sometimes in stairways, causing deep injury. He was so worried about future assaults that he was seen throwing up on the school's front lawn.

Trevor, the Chicago Four, and the mentally challenged people you've seen assaulted tell us that if an uncompromised mind and body are the final criteria determining what makes us fully human and worthy of human dignity, all dark omens become possible.

My friend Garry, who does a killer Elvis impression, has Down syndrome. He has shown me a kinder and more winsome side of what it means to be human. He recently asked me to sit with him and share "our thoughts and feelings." I still smile when I think about our time together.

But is Garry fully human? It hurts me to even write this question, because I know how much happiness he bestows upon the world. But I have to write it in order to help us understand the mind of the Chicago Four, the bullies at your child's school, your work, and in your family. A surprising number of them say no.

Garry, like the eighteen-year-old young man from Chicago, is fully human; not because of his mind, but because, although we are all different, we are all created in the same image of the same God. There are no children of a lesser god, just a minority of arrogant and sinister bullies in great need of humility, but who weaponize differences to feel superior and to ridicule and terrorize the most vulnerable among us.

Notes

[1] Justin Taylor, "Driscoll's Confession on Pride, " *The Gospel Coaltion* (blog), November 9, 2007, https://www.thegospelcoalition.org/blogs/justin-taylor /driscolls-confession-on-pride/.

[2] Jimmy Dodd (president of PastorServe), personal interview with author.

[3] Barbara Coloroso, *Extraordinary Evil: A Short Walk to Genocide* (New York: Nation Books, 2007), 59.

[4] "Confessions of a Real Mean Girl," *The Protectors*, July 17, 2012, https:// theprotectors.org/2012/07/17/confessions-of-a-real-mean-girl. "Confessions of a Real Mean Girl, Part II," *The Protectors*, July 31, 2012, https://theprotectors .org/2012/07/31/confessions-of-a-real-mean-girl-part-ii/.

[5] Jean M. Twenge and W. Keith Campbell, *The Narcissism Epidemic: Living in the Age of Entitlement* (New York: Atria Books:) 360.

[6] Twenge and Campbell, *The Narcissism Epidemic*, 69.

[7] Ronald Schouten and James Silver, *Almost a Psychopath: Do I (or Does Someone I Know) Have a Problem with Empathy?* (Center City, MN: Harvard Medical School, 2012), 128.

[8] Schouten and Silver, *Almost a Psychopath*, 128.

[9] Schouten and Silver, *Almost a Psychopath*, 8.

[10] "Narcissistic Personality Disorder," *Psychology Today*, March 6, 2018, https://www.psychologytoday.com/us/conditions/narcissistic-personality -disorder.

[11] Bonnie Pritchett, "Darrin Patrick Commits to Restoration Process," *World*, April 15, 2016, https://world.wng.org/2016/04/darrin_patrick_commits_to _restoration_process.

[12] Jon Sutton, Peter K. Smith, and John Swettenham, "Bullying and 'Theory of Mind': A Critique of the 'Social Skills Deficit' View of Anti-Social Behaviour," *Social Development* 8, no. 1 (1999): 124.

[13] Drake Baer, "Why Humble People Make Better Decisions," *Thrive Global*, March 20, 2017, https://journal.thriveglobal.com/why-humble-people-make -better-decisions-d18e6ad6180a.

[14] David Brooks, *The Road to Character* (New York: Random House, 2015), iBooks.

"I Found Someone Else"

While speaking at a public elementary school in Idaho, something I said jogged the principal's memory.

"In October," she said, "I noticed that a boy wasn't bullying another boy like he did last year in fifth grade." She said that she congratulated the sixth grader for being a kinder person, hoping she was reinforcing his better behavior.

"He looked at me with a big smile and said, 'I know. I found someone else.'" She told me that he said this with pride and without a shred of introspection or shame. He said it with excitement in his voice as he looked forward to a new school year of new possibilities of making this boy miserable, the way a person might look forward to going to a concert or a great movie on a Friday night. Like many children who bully, he had selected his new target in September and laid into him by October.

A school counselor at a Christian school for nearly twenty years says she has never been able to get one serial bully to change his or her heart. "They curtail their behavior just enough so they don't get kicked out. But they don't even try to be truly good or decent." And their parents, she said with mild disgust, thwarted her good work. "They oppose my efforts to help their children. They fight me continually, making excuses and even lying for their children."

Sometimes it takes a foolish kid, blinded by both pride and pleasure, to reveal the unvarnished truth about bullying to us adults. About how it's a moral crime of practice, not opportunity, and how predatory it really is. And it takes a veteran counselor at a Christian school to help us see how hard, if not impossible, it is to change the mind and soul of a serial bully through appeals to the Golden Rule. "If men were angels," wrote James Madison, "no government would be necessary." If children were angels, there would be no need for an anti-bullying month.

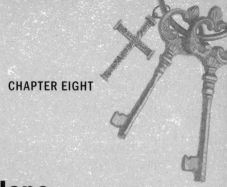

CHAPTER EIGHT

Love, Light, and Hope in the Theater of Bullying

Our world is desperate for Christians who know how to respond to the heart of the world rather than with the heart of the world. —Don McLaughlin

NOW THAT WE HAVE A BETTER UNDERSTANDING OF THE R-RATED THEATER OF BULLYING, INCLUDING HOW BULLIES really think and feel, it's time to provide real solutions that go beyond playing nice and instead create actual love, light, and hope. Let's start with targets, the group that needs the most help.

During a recent Community Night presentation in Southern California, I was asked a question that I've received many times, and which is usually asked by men more than women: "Why doesn't the target just stand up to the bully? That would end it right there." There is solid logic to this statement, and it's usually followed up with how the adult who asked this question stood up to a bully when he was young, and how they later became friends, sometimes best friends.

We train people how to treat us; unfortunately, serial targets can be poor trainers—in part because they have been given a very nice but unwise script to follow. Many serial targets will never even tell the bully to stop, which is unfortunate because telling the bully to stop in an assertive voice and manner can be an effective, though not foolproof, first-line defense against bullying.

Yet as you know by now, bullies select those who don't push back.

Saying "No! Stop!" while looking the bully in the eye, or physically standing up for themselves, can mortify many serial targets. I worked with one serial target whose parents required him to look his bully in the eye and tell him to stop. His response? He stopped going to school. Some targets won't have it within them to defend themselves until they reach adulthood. Some may never have it in them. It's even worse for some kids who grow up with a so-called "Christian" script, like Peretti, that says self-defense is wrong and sinful.

Having helped many targets, I know how averse they are to standing up for themselves. So I've found that it's best to frame what's happening to them not in terms of combat or war, but resistance, which sounds and feels more kind and achievable to them and their families.

Resistance without War

We have three general paths to choose from when responding to provocation and abuse: the passive response, the aggressive response, and, our best choice, the assertive response. Many Christians see the passive response as the only viable response. I hope by now that we've seen that this is not only false, but may also be a sinful and dangerous response.

More so, passive people may be gracious people, but their grace doesn't come from a place of strength. It comes from the weakness of wanting to please everyone, of fearing the opinions of others more than being concerned with what God expects from them. Such people may show grace to others, but they are often untruthful, so they fail to create healthy boundaries for themselves and others, and their dishonesty is a sin as well. It's been my experience that the passive response to bullying is advocated more by mothers than fathers.

An aggressive approach is usually advocated by fathers more than mothers. With the aggressive approach, the target is told to punch the bully as hard as they can, return an insult for an insult, or some related behavior. I believe in the value of righteous violence, that a person has both a right and a freedom to defend their value and worth from those, like serial bullies, who want to take them away. As mentioned earlier, our concept of violence comes from our concept of *violation*. I don't believe targets of abusive behavior violate abusers when they defend themselves, provided their self-defense isn't inordinate.

Given what I know about serial targets, I don't believe that telling such a child to physically defend himself or herself is teaching them to "use violence to solve their problems." This is because such children are not aggressive by nature, so it's not within their nature to want to use violence to get their way in other theaters of life. And though using physical force is not innately wrong, it also gets us off the mark. That's because about 80 percent of bullying is verbal, not physical. The sooner we teach our children the art of resistance without war, the higher they will fly in life as children and adults.

Another problem with the aggressive approach is that asking nonaggressive children to be aggressive is a very large leap for them—like asking them to run a mile in under four minutes because others have done it. Some just can't do it and won't make this leap. A much better solution for them is to train them in the ways of assertiveness.

It's important that I add a nuanced point here. I think training a child in the art of physical self-defense falls into the assertive path written about in this section because doing so is filtered power, which I call *strength*. It's refined aggression where a child is trained to use physical force only in specific incidents. But more than that, martial arts, boxing, wrestling, and related training can remove a lot of fear of assault, which is no small gift in a theater where weakness invites aggression among the malevolent. This draining of fear allows confidence (not arrogance) to grow into other areas as well, such as more assertive facial expressions, gait, and other aspects of body language that we'll get into later. Such confidence alone makes it much more likely that they may never have to use physical force in the first place.

Our goal throughout this section is to resist bullying without becoming abusive bullies or passive, people-pleasing doormats. It's the assertive way that is in line with Christian morality and behavior and is obtainable by most serial targets. To achieve it in most cases most of the time, it's helping targets express a confident and strong personality, even when they might not feel strong and confident inside (at least at first).

Fake It till You Make It

There's a joke that goes like this: the meek may have inherited the earth, but first they'll ask for permission. The meeker personality doesn't assert itself very well. It radiates to others "I won't contest you if you want to contest me." I believe God has created a path toward freedom for such people who are often targets, giving them and their families more hope, courage, and control than they realize. And it's simple: change your body language.

Nonassertive body language can be the first trait bullies seek in their targets—as do violent criminals. Body language experts warn that criminals key in on submissive body language, such as a downward gaze, slumped posture, and "a gait that lacks organized movement and flowing motion," which "signals fear or physical vulnerability." Even sadder, they warn that "women with passive, submissive personalities are most likely to be raped—and they tend to wear body-concealing clothing, such as high necklines, long pants and sleeves, and multiple layers."[1] Criminals, like bullies, target the nice and humble.

Dr. Albert Mehrabian, a professor of psychology at UCLA, concludes that spoken words consists of a mere 7 percent of all communication, 35 percent is conveyed through tone of voice, and the remaining 58 percent through body language.[2] I see detrimental body language in every school I talk to. These students make little eye contact. And when they do, it's nervous, darting, and erratic. Studies show that they exhibit fearful body language *before* they are attacked by bullies. Targets often do not smile before the first incident of bullying either. They take shorter strides, and their shoulders are hunched more forward and higher toward their ears when compared to their peers. When standing with their peers, their legs are closer together because nonassertive people, unknowingly, remain small and don't take up space the way confident people do. When standing, they sometimes shuffle from foot to foot, the way inexperienced public speakers stand due to nervousness. While consulting on the movie *Courage in a Time of Fear,* I was talking with one of the directors between scenes. A group of high school boys were standing in a near perfect circle except for one boy. He was half a step outside the circle. The two boys next to him weren't pinching him out either. They were leaving room for him to enter. But he wouldn't. He shuffled from foot to foot, looking down, itchy and uncomfortable.

"If I were a bully," I told the director, "That's who I would target." I told him that I would test him first. I would walk by him and "accidentally" hit his shoulder with mine. If he withered, I would know that I found my target. I would initiate the usual steps to crime against him (which are explored later in this chapter).

The word *assert* comes from the words *claim, affirm,* and *to join*—behaviors serial targets do not practice, but they will with coaching. They don't assert themselves physically, verbally, or through body language. But the great news is that this can change. A leader in the realm of positive body language is Harvard's Amy Cuddy, creator of "power posing," and whose TEDTalk on the topic remains one of the most popular.

Those who power pose strike a confident, not arrogant, pose. When standing, their chin is level, they have a pleasant and inviting look on their face, they make steady eye contact, and look away when appropriate. They have a relaxed and open demeanor or air to them. They stand with their legs apart, sometimes in what is called the "cowboy stance," with one leg to the side and in front of the other. When growing up in the seventies, many rock stars struck this pose on the covers of their albums because it shows confidence. Those who power pose sometimes put one or two hands on their hips. They take longer strides when walking and have a relaxed gait. When seated, they take up space, sometimes putting their arm around the chair near them—compare this with targets, who remain small when seated, sometimes putting both their arms in their lap.

Here's where God has shown even more grace to the timid. Cuddy's research reveals that if someone strikes a powerful pose before a mirror for just two minutes (think Wonder Woman with her legs slightly apart, hands on hips, shoulders back, and assertive look on her face), the chemicals associated with self-confidence increase. That's just after two minutes, something any child can do before school at home. There is reason to believe that putting a slight smile on your face does something similar. To train targets to put a slight smile on their face, Cuddy suggests having them say the funny phrase "cheese whiz" to themselves, and then telling them to hold it.[3]

While speaking at a Christian summer camp in Scranton, Pennsylvania, I was begged by a father to work with his fourteen-year-old son Kevin, a target of serial bullying. I could see why: In the 150-watt world of adolescent children, he was a 25-watt bulb. Though very bright, he moved slowly, slouched, was slack-jawed, didn't make eye contact, and mumbled—an ideal target.

I didn't have much time to work with him as we walked across the campus, so I put him in a kind of assertiveness boot camp. I coached him on how to walk and talk more confidently, pulling his shoulders back but staying relaxed at the same time. I had him pause from time to time and close his eyes, let his shoulders drop, and put a slight smile on his face. I had him visualize seeing himself walking and talking in a more relaxed way. I had him speak a little louder and over-pronounce his words since he was so used to under-pronouncing. (For a great example of a person who pronounces well, watch and listen to Ryan Seacrest.)

We role-played. I pretended to bully him, and he responded with "whatever." I trained him to say it with confidence and put a dismissive, *I-Don't-Care-What-You-Think* look on his face. We talked about the importance of friendships, and how they can keep bullies away.

Kevin was motivated, but he struggled at first. But I wish I had recorded his transformation, because it was remarkable and personally rewarding to me. He bloomed before my eyes in less than fifteen minutes of help. He literally looked and acted more confident.

When we got to his cabin, I asked him, "How do you feel?"

"I feel great, but this feels weird," he said.

"That right!" I said. "It does feel weird at first; but over time, it will feel normal and great the more you do it."

Yet people object to this training. They say that no child should have to change who they are to please a bully. I share some of this belief. I wish a kid like Kevin could "be who he is," that he could walk the way he walks and appear the way he wants to appear without concern. Yet in youth culture, each decision carries with it consequences that aren't as dire in adult culture. Their social pressure chamber is greater and more restrictive, and wishful thinking won't change the setting. How a child is perceived by his peers has extreme ramifications that can lead to profound isolation, humiliation, and related abuse from peers. We're derelict as adults if we don't help them surmount what is within their power to surmount.

This was the case with Trevor, a ninth grader at a high school in California who hired me to coach him to appear less attractive to his bully. It helped that Trevor was a gifted actor who had earned the starring role in the school's play, which sadly opened his life to increased jealousy and envy. I had him study actor Ryan Gosling, comparing his assertive body language in *Crazy Stupid Love* to his passive body language in *Lars and the Real Girl*. He put his acting skills to work right away. I helped him practice what I call the all-knowing smile, a look that tells bullies that what you say and do doesn't matter to me—even when it does. It's a look that says "whatever" without saying it (more on verbal self-defense later). Trevor's more assertive body language told his bully that he would no longer be pushed around. Another great example of passive-to-confident body language is found in Conor, the main character in the movie *Sing Street*.

Parents and guardians can conduct a short "interview." This is where a target stands and answers a series of light-hearted questions (What is your favorite food? What is your favorite color? and so on) while being recorded before coaching on how to appear more assertive. Then the target is given the assertiveness tips found in this section and asked the same questions while being recorded.

The goal isn't to change the content of the answers, but how the target answers, how he holds himself while listening and talking. My experience has been that within minutes, the target can appear noticeably more confident. And you will be able to prove this because you have recorded the entire "interview." You will have a before-and-after video right there, and you will be better able to celebrate your child's progress.

If targets don't respond to the bullying they are subjected to, they may never get their power back, and with it some agency over their lives. Sure, they or their bully may move away, graduate, or change, but targets will be haunted by their bully's ongoing campaign of cruelty. They experience loss, sometimes profound loss, and it's too much for some, who take their lives.

Although most targets live, they struggle to really live—the bland gaze in their eyes is the same as that of soldiers returning from war, because their condition is more than stress; it's *traumatic* stress. Their wounding kills their spirit and causes them to recoil from circumstances that might usher the possibility of pain and risk, like love, although they long for love just like everyone else. But fear and fear-filled memories can thwart them from finding it. Some will believe they don't deserve love, either from God or the person of their dreams. They are more likely to live their lives with eyes down and shoulders slumped—they may even wince when receiving a compliment—all signs of battered self-esteem that sex traffickers also look for. They typically won't insert themselves into conversations—including job interviews where the interviewer can tell the person is smart but, for reasons they can't understand, just won't step up and proclaim anything, even if the job depends on it and their family depends on them. They are more likely to become codependent and look to others to fill their many inner voids. They will likely believe the abusive spouse who tells them that to push back is to be "bad"—just like their school bullies told them. They are great candidates for gaslighting in all major theaters of life, and for the rest of their lives.

Targets often need to be coached on how to advocate for themselves. One way to see where the coaching needs to start is to ask a target if he or she has told the bully to stop. It seems simple, and we usually assume he or she has. But a surprising number of targets won't even tell the bully to leave them alone. When I ask them why they haven't, they usually tell me, "I don't know," or "I don't want to." Many times, they do not give an answer.

Here's the clarifying truth: telling a bully to stop isn't unloving or uncaring. It's not violent, mean, or cruel. It's not bad, and it's certainly not unchristian since Jesus verbally defended himself against the guard of the high priest who slapped him in the face. He also told one of the disciples who was bullying Mary to "Leave her alone!" There is no viable moral code that would prohibit a person from telling a bully to stop. So it's not about violating a moral code. More times than not, it's about a target's reluctance to self-advocate.

Friendships

I addressed assertive body language to ward off bullying before addressing the necessity of friendships for a reason: it makes targets more attractive to potential friends. This is important because many targets don't know how they are perceived by others. They need to be saved from their own self-defeating habits and behaviors. They know that their clothing can create a perception about who they are, but they don't yet understand how the person inside the clothing holds herself makes an even bigger impression—for better or worse.

Friendships are a frontline defense against bullying, since bullies often seek out isolated prey. But friendships can be a challenge for targets because they often fall on the nonassertive side of life, making them appear less friendly. Over-parenting can play a role in this inability as well, since children whose parents intervene, override, and make most of their decisions for them can have difficulty extending their will in the world of adolescence.

Beneficial body language is an essential precondition for friendships. Without it, a target's genuine effort to make friends can be thwarted pretty quickly. This can be a very expensive mistake that can be avoided.

Here are some common ways that friendships are made and grown. (When discussing the following with a target, keep the conversation light. I have found as a coach and father of three that discussing heavier topics with a light touch happens best when on a walk or a drive, playing catch, throwing a Frisbee, or kicking a ball around.)

1. Help targets spend more face-to-face time with others. This may appear obvious, but it's not to many targets who may spend too much time playing video games, which numbs pain but limits their ability to grow the friendships needed to ward off bullying.

2. At lunchtime, help targets try not to wiggle their way onto the "popular" table, a common mistake for new students that is viewed by classmates as intrusive, offensive, and even unforgiveable. Instead, encourage them to sit at a table with at least two other students their age, building friendships from there.

3. Join an organization, sports team, church, or club with students who have common interests. As a coach of competitive soccer for nearly twenty years, I have

witnessed a common misconception about sports, where players believe they have to be a standout player in order to be "popular." Rather, it's a player's personality that is usually most important: open, considerate, humorous, and confident, but also relaxed. They don't need to start to be popular.

4. Help targets make eye contact and smile more. Avoid squinting (get glasses or contacts), looking bored, frowning, folding your arms, hanging out in a corner, or appearing blankly deadpan or slack-jawed. Such habits may make targets look troubled or disinterested when they really aren't. Also, help targets avoid a monotone manner. Help them vary their pitch when speaking.

5. Help targets make small talk. Keep the conversation light and cheery. Even if targets complain about something, make sure the topic is something both the target and potential friend are dissatisfied with.

6. Help targets introduce themselves at the end of the conversation. It can be as simple as saying, "Oh, by the way, my name is . . ." The other person will usually do the same. Remember the person's name! If targets show that they remember particulars from past conversations, they will look intelligent, caring, and genuinely friendly.

7. Help initiate get-togethers. Targets can chat their hearts out, but it won't get them friends if they don't create the opportunity for another conversation or meeting.

8. Help targets avoid pressuring others to be their friends too quickly. This is especially important for kids who are new to a school or neighborhood, and who try to push themselves into circles of friendships too soon, and in the wrong way.

9. Remind targets to not be "fair-weather friends," only maintaining the relationship when it's fun or enjoyable at the time. And emphasize that they should never complain about their friend to other people. When possible, parents and guardians should give examples from their own life when they said something bad about a friend behind their back, and how it harmed the relationship later.

10. Help targets become good listeners. For example, many think that in order to be seen as "friend material," they have to appear very interesting all the time. Far more important, however, is the ability to show they're interested in others.

11. Help targets emphasize their good and unique qualities—not the bothersome ones. Help them use humor if they're good at it, but make sure not to attack others with it, especially through sarcasm.

12. Finally, help targets keep in mind that making and maintaining friendships is more of an art than a science. Sometimes, despite our best intentions, friendships just don't work out, and this is true for adults as well. The real imperative is to just be friendly on a regular basis, because more times than not, relationships will work out.

This quote from C. S. Lewis has helped a number of targets get a better understanding of what friendship is about: "Friendship is born at that moment when one man says to another: 'What! You too? I thought that no one but myself . . .'"[4]

Likability is essential to friendships as well as success in life in general. A University of Massachusetts study found that managers were willing to accept an auditor's argument with no supporting evidence if he or she was likeable.[5] Another study found that just one in two thousand unlikeable leaders are considered effective.[6]

Travis Bradberry, writing for the *Huffington Post*, lists common unlikeable behaviors. They run the spectrum from targets not trying enough, trying too hard, and sometimes just not being aware of how they're perceived by others.

1. Humble-bragging. This is where people brag about themselves behind a "mask of self-deprecation." For example, the girl who calls herself a nerd because she wants to call attention to how smart she is.
2. Being too serious.
3. Not asking enough questions in conversations.
4. Emotional hijackings, such as "throwing things, screaming, making people cry." Targets are prone to public displays of pain and anguish, which can include lashing out at others—behaviors we see from Hannah Baker in the series *13 Reasons Why*.
5. Whipping out your phone during conversations and other together times. Best to wait for an ebb in the conversation when others look at their phones as well.
6. Name-dropping. Targets will do this in order to move up the social ladder, but it can backfire very quickly.
7. Gossiping. This can be another attempt to gain entrance into a circle of friends. Eventually, people come to realize that if you're gossiping about others, you're gossiping about them too.
7. Having a closed mind by dismissing and judging people too quickly, a trait of highly opinionated people.
8. Sharing too much, too early. This can trip up even older adolescent targets, because sharing is something friends do. But sharing too much too early appears insensitive to the other person—and might hint that you are high-maintenance.

9. Sharing too much on social media. Studies have shown that people who over-share on social media do so because they crave acceptance, and the Pew Research Center has revealed that this over-sharing works against them by making people dislike them.[7]

Verbal Comebacks

Christ forbids us from seeking revenge, for taking an eye for an eye and tooth for a tooth. The same is true for targets when it comes to derogatory and insulting words, by far the most prevalent form of bullying. We are not allowed to return an insult for an insult, but this sure doesn't mean we cannot defend ourselves verbally, even forcefully.

Some parents will tell their children to not respond at all, believing that any response will just make matters worse, or that by responding, their children will "lower themselves to the bully's level." It is true that not responding to a bully's deliberate provocation can help thwart bullying, since the bully did not get the rise she wanted out of a target. But at the same time, this can be dangerous advice since not responding can be perceived as a weakness, motivating bullies to continue and increase their attacks.

There is an assertive way to stand up verbally called "fogging." This is when a person responds to provocation with a message of his own that often does not address the initial provocation directly, or at all. We'll get to examples of fogging shortly.

But fogging is an uncomfortable practice for many targets, especially Christian targets who believe that they owe everyone, including bullies, candor. Otherwise, they worry that they are being rude, unkind, and even mean. Yet bullies are dangerous and harmful people. We do not owe such people access to our lives. We owe confidants our candor, not abusers.

There are at least two truths found in the book of Proverbs that support this claim. One tells us that a fool utters all that he thinks, but a wise man keep his thoughts to himself (Prov. 29:11). The other explains how fools show their annoyance at once, but the prudent overlook an insult (Prov. 12:16). Both tell us that concealing how we think and feel not only is Christian, but to do otherwise is foolish.

We have a great example of this in the life of Jesus, who rarely responded to entrapping questions directly. He often responded with a question of his own designed to get to the truth, and to put his accusers on their heels.

Some parents, still trying to avoid the obvious need for effective verbal comebacks, will encourage their child to use humor, even self-deprecating humor, to get the bullies to stop, even when their child isn't funny. This is problematic for two reasons. First, if a child isn't known for being humorous, telling them to be so is an extremely difficult task. So difficult that it is an unfair and burdensome request. Humor is a highly nuanced ability. It can take years to develop not just the content of humor but also its exacting delivery. And second, self-deprecating humor can easily backfire in the hands of a bully, who may use the intentional putdown as ammo later against the target.

Instead, we need to teach targets to respond without directly responding to the attack through the following phrases that work best. Help them memorize the top three that they like, and practice saying them to another person in a way that says to the bully, *What you say doesn't matter to me.* This probably isn't true, but targets need to pretend that it's true. Tell the target in your life: Practice saying your favorite phrases in an assertive but relaxed matter. Put a look on your face that says you have way better things to do with your life. Put a slight smile on our face and, at the same time, give a look of rejection with your eyes, like you just heard something really, really dumb. This is because you have. What the bully is saying to you is a deliberate lie. It's false. It is normal and healthy to reject falsehood.

These words and statements include, but aren't limited to, the following:

"Whatever."
"That's cruel."
"This is over."
"That's mean."
"This is a waste of time."
"That's sexist."
"Interesting."
"You have an interesting life."
"That's racist."
"Great."
"Right."
"That's harrassment."
"That's not true at all. Excuse me."
"People like you say anything."
"The things you say. Take care."
"Whatever. See you later."
"It's true because I said it's true."
"That's beneath both of us."
"I don't need this."
"Take care."

Some of these phrases are better suited for younger students than older students and vice versa. Some require humor, which can be difficult for some students to pull off well.

I have used "It's true because I said it's true" to multiple bullies, and it has stopped them in their tracks—in part because it's so unexpected from someone who had previously been under their thumb. Back then, before I understood why bullies behave the way they do, I tried to reason with him, thinking I was embroiled in some degree of misunderstanding. I was outgunned, on my heels, confused, and full of emotional pain. It dawned on me during that heated moment that unlike me, he had no interest in reaching compromise or resolution. He wanted to humiliate me. Again. To this day, I'm not sure where this phrase came from, but it came out of my lips. He did not anticipate this statement, and chances are, neither will your bully.

I spoke truth to dark power, which was the beginning of the end of a relationship that, looking back, should have ended years prior. Here's one reason why it ended: with this one phrase, I created my own storm cloud, full of electricity. Truth can do that. I didn't just slam on the brakes—I put the conversation in reverse. I took territory in this battle to stake out a functioning level of respect, which is essential to all authentic relationships. At that moment, he no longer had the upper hand, which was intolerable to him, so *he* ended the relationship.

Of all these phrases, we highly recommend "Whatever," because it's dismissive without becoming a bully. But these words alone aren't enough. Something else is essential. After saying what you need to say, leave. Don't hang around and engage in some drawn out conversation with someone who is hellbent on tripping you up. If possible, say your favorite phrase while you're still walking. Bullies need two factors in their favor, just the way other criminals do: time and location. Don't let the bully choose either of them if possible. Don't let the bully choose the battlefield. One way to do this is to keep moving.

Three-Part Experience with Bullying

Now that we have the right mindset, body language, and words and phrases ready to go, it's time to analyze what a usual encounter with a bully looks like, because those who are forewarned are fore-armed. The usual encounter takes a predictable, three-part process. By knowing this process, you can find its weaknesses and exploit them to your advantage.

It helps to view an experience with a bully as similar to driving a car through a sharp corner at speed. You don't have to be a Formula-One racer to know that corners have three parts: the entrance, the corner itself, and the exit, or bottom of the corner.

An experience with a bully is similar. I call the three parts the three Es. There is an *entrance*, usually into a room, but it could be at a more open venue, such as a sports park. There's the *encounter* with the bully. And then there is the *exit*, where the target leaves the theater of bullying, hopefully with success.

Targets do themselves a massive solid if they enter the venue well, which sets them up for success. To do so, they and those coaching them must respect the process itself, the way racers respect corners—because although corners are where races are won, they are also where crashes happen. Similarly, targets and those coaching them must be serious (not somber) about the three-part encounter with a bully.

Yet this is where most targets and their advisors fail, because they don't really believe, deep down, that the bully is a nemesis. Yet bullies devise new ways to make targets miserable, or as the Bible says, "In his arrogance the wicked man hunts down the weak, who are caught in the schemes he devises" (Ps. 10:2 NIV).

Bullies lie and ask leading, misleading, and entrapping questions. Worse, nice people believe they owe the bully an answer, when the Bible tells us we shouldn't. Many bullies are willfully unteachable. This makes them what the Bible calls a "fool"—someone who not only refuses wisdom; he scorns it. And in Proverbs, we are told, "Do not answer a fool according to his folly, or you yourself will be just like him" (Prov. 26:4 NIV). It is foolish and folly (a word that comes from *madness*) to play the bully's game.

A final warning before explaining the first part of our encounter with a bully: be wise with whom you share your game plan of resistance without war. Generally speaking, do not share it with your friends unless you are absolutely confident they will not tell anyone. This game plan is too juicy for most people to keep quiet about, especially adolescents. If your bully and his or her support staff find out about it, your chances of success are probably blown. They will likely use this information to humiliate you even more. Share only with your parents and/or guardians instead.

The Entrance

Targets should enter the theater or venue of bullying with confidence, even if it's fake at first. One way to spur confidence is to enter the theater with a friend if possible. Don't look around wildly or nervously for your bully. Relax by dropping your shoulders and putting a friendly look on your face. Practice this well before you enter the room.

To the best of your ability, pretend that the bully doesn't matter. I'm not advocating mean-mugging here. Targets want to give the impression that their lives are so rich and wonderful that the bully just doesn't fit into their schedule or register on their social radar.

Our mouths sometimes get dry when nervous, which leads to even more feelings of nervousness. Anticipate this by making sure to have a few pieces of gum with you. It will keep your mouth from drying out and can give you a more relaxed and confident look as well. One thing singers do when their mouths dry out is lightly bite the end of their tongue, which stimulates moisture as well.

Give an all-knowing smile that says, "I'm here; you can't harm me; my life is great." Remember how weakness and even kindness invite aggression from certain people? The all-knowing smile combats it for you. (Again, think of Ryan Gosling in *Crazy Stupid Love*. Will Smith and Emma Stone are really good at creating this kind of smile as well.)

Don't stand facing your bully. Rather, keep the bully just off your shoulder in order to keep an eye on them without looking directly at them. Make very limited eye contact with the bully (or better yet, none at all—at least when you enter the theater).

Stand with your legs slightly further apart than usual, which gives you a more confident and balanced appearance. Work the room. Strike up conversations with others, but don't bad mouth the bully when you do. Remember: people in social settings care more about comfort than fairness and truth. Telling others the truth about bullies makes others so uncomfortable that they will bad-mouth you instead. It's how this world works most of the time, unfortunately. Unless the person you're talking to is a great friend, he or she will probably tell someone close to the bully, if not the bully herself. Don't criticize the bully to someone who is not a true confidant.

The Experience

Chances are, the bully or bullies will notice you are behaving differently, so expect to be attacked and prepare for it ahead of time by realizing that surprise equals control. There are two ways to prepare for a bully's attack, similar to how to prepare for a criminal attack. When preparing to commit a crime, a criminal usually chooses the right time and location for them but not their target. So expect bullies to at least try to take advantage of both as well. Try to make it difficult for them by limiting your exposure to timing and location.

Don't be alone, if possible, and don't allow yourself to be cornered. This may mean avoiding bathrooms, so go to the bathroom before you get to the venue of frequent bullying. Also try to stay away from the edges of a group, if possible.

But if this doesn't work, and the bully and his minions eventually get to you, here's what to do:

Don't initiate a handshake or a hug. If they extend their hand or want to hug you and others are present, shake their hand firmly, and quickly end the handshake. End the hug early as well. Don't express anger or annoyance in larger social settings, because even though you have the right to express anger and related emotions, doing so will make others uncomfortable, and you don't want to be the one making people uncomfortable. You, not the bully, will be seen as the bad guy.

Keep your all-knowing smile going, and do the best you can to relax (or at least appear relaxed). Stand or sit askew to the bully since facing someone is a sign of respect, the way you might stand or sit straight toward a police officer or principal at school. This won't be obvious to those around you, or even to the bully right away. But it sends a message.

Make quick eye contact, then end it, doing the best you can to look uninterested. Continuous and invested eye contact is a sign of extraordinary respect that is given to friends. A bully does not deserve this level of respect from you.

If hit with a snarky or otherwise injurious comment, pretend it doesn't bother you. Scoff, roll your eyes, and/or shake your head—whatever is most comfortable to you.

Don't partake in a drawn-out conversation. Instead, say one of the words or phrases listed earlier in this chapter that you've been practicing, then leave whenever possible to where other people are so you don't get cornered again.

The Exit

If you demonstrate this kind of resistance without war, you will have surprised the bully and those under his or her spell. And as written previously, surprise equals control and power. Your bully, bright or not, will sense this power shift, and may work quickly to get you back under his or her control. Your enemy bully will most likely bad mouth you even more.

Leave.

I can't make this point strongly enough. You have won a victory, so don't let your bully snatch defeat from the mouth of your victory. You have won a battle, but not the war, probably. More battles of training others how to treat you are likely coming, and you will have to steel yourself for them with both courage and wisdom. But at this moment, you have restructured part of the social landscape of your life, and the bully will want to get back whatever power you've taken. Make it difficult; so difficult that with the aid of time and physical distance, your victory can't be taken from you.

If the event isn't over, leave early if you can. Do so without being noticed much, and make a quick exit. Don't linger while being picked up by a parent. If you're driving, get your car keys out early and don't delay. Park in an easy-to-see place, away from edges or corners. Park under a light when possible. Back in so you can leave even more quickly. If you're being picked up, don't wait by standing still in one place. Have the person text you that they are there, and walk with confidence to the car and go.

Why am I saying all this? Because your bully and his support crew may try to get a shot at you before you leave. Don't let them stop you. If the bully wants to "talk," say, "Gotta go. Take care." Walk away, ride away, drive away.

If you want to comment about the event on social media, say you had a great time and don't mention the bully (or bullies) by name. Pretend that you had the time of your life and that you're life is great, even if it's not.

Helping a Wounded Spirit

People need water before they need food. I learned something similar during a kingdom-minded retreat in Belize hosted by Roy Goble, author of *Junkyard Wisdom*. We explored God's love and will for justice, and how beleaguered people need hope before they can digest love. This is because they need to have some belief that they have a viable future. Otherwise, love doesn't take root in them the way we want it to.

Targets need help growing a more hopeful and joyful outlook on life. Consider implementing these helpful changes in behavior and activities:

1. Renew activities that have brought enjoyment and pleasure in the past. Sometimes looking through old photographs, Facebook pages, and so on can help jar memories.
2. Remind targets about their existing friendships and help grow them into even stronger friendships.
3. Sometimes a change of scenery does wonders. Go to a new place. Get out of your town for a while.
4. Remind them that God loves them, and what is happening to them is not his will since he has no part in wickedness and evil.
5. Bring humor into your home. Consume humorous movies, books, YouTube videos, and more.
6. Expose or reintroduce targets to stories of courage and victory, including books, movies, and so on.
7. Physical exercise is proven to help alleviate blueness and depression. It reduces anxiety and gets good feelings going again. Help your child implement a physical exercise program, either on their own or, ideally, with a friend or potential friend.

8. Journaling is also proven to bring greater hope and clarity to a target's struggling mind and spirit.

9. Help your child be good at one activity that ideally brings him or her into contact with potential friends, such as sports, music, theater, and so on. Children who are good at one activity are less likely to be bullied and have greater self-regard as well.

Avoid Bullying Hot Spots

Part of positioning, as mentioned earlier, is that bullies like to hang out in places where bullying is easier. We call these places "bullying hot spots." Their existence is typically obvious to adults, but not for some targets. This is because many targets have so much fear and anxiety going through them that they don't see the theater of bullying clearly. This fear takes on a cataract-like quality, clouding their perception of what's really happening. Targets often give their bullies an almost god-like power, believing that they possess a kind of omnipotence. This can stem from what Dr. Townsend described earlier as "learned helplessness," where the target believes in the three deadly Ps: that their situation is *personal*, *prevalent*, and *permanent*. They believe it's their fault, that it happens to people all the time, and that the situation will not change. They need adults to lift them out of this mire of hopelessness and deceit. This is done by helping them realize that bullying doesn't happen everywhere and at all times. It happens in places that favor the bully, such as venues that have limited visibility for authority, a time and location lock (meaning the target has to be somewhere, like get to a class on time), and an opportunity to strike quickly.

Sometimes avoiding these hot spots is all a child needs to do to stop being bullied, which is what happened with Caleb. I don't know how he got my cellphone number, but he did. Caleb called me just before I was going to have dinner with my family. This fourth grader was well spoken and really wanted my help with bullying. So I said, "Caleb, I'm just about to have dinner with my family, but let's do this. Get your mom on the phone."

I asked Caleb where the bullying was taking place. He told me he was being pushed off a four-foot concrete wall at lunchtime by sixth graders.

"Caleb, do you need to be at that wall at lunchtime?" I asked.

"No," he said. "I just liked hanging out there until those boys came over."

"Do you get bullied anywhere else at school?" I asked.

"No, just there," he said.

"Caleb," I said. "Don't go near the four-foot wall at lunchtime."

I checked back with him two weeks later and the bullying had ended.

Sometimes it's that simple.

Be Good at Something

Children who get bullied are sometimes on the bottom rung of the social ladder, where kids are known as "nobodies." This isn't true in the eyes of God and descent people, but it is true in youth culture, even Christian youth culture.

So parents and related guardians, assess your child's interests, then help your child explore those interests. Since targets can be shy, you will probably have to push (not shove) them in this direction. Consider one example from my life: I awoke one morning and was told, two weeks before my first practice, that I was signed up on a soccer team. I was just ten years old, and I was furious. But my parents knew I needed to get out of the house more and socialize with kids my own age. I hated soccer at first. I just stood there with my hands in my pockets afraid to receive the ball because I feared making a mistake. But then something clicked, and I became one of the better players. The game of soccer would later enrich my life for decades. I was an average-grade student who had no thought of going to college, which I thought was for other, smarter kids. But toward my senior year, and as a captain of the soccer team, I began to think, "If I can excel at this game, maybe I can use similar skills to get into college."

I was good at one thing, the beautiful game, and it helped me feel better about myself and gave me esteem among my peers, which protected me from bullying. Our experience at The Protectors has shown us that though there are many options of things to be good at, one of the more popular options is a musical instrument, especially the acoustic guitar, which is very portable and fairly inexpensive. After talking to many targets, I've learned that there is something about the guitar that does more than bring an adolescent competency; it has a way of soothing their soul as well. Many of these former targets became composers, putting their feelings, including their pain, into lyrics and melodies—reducing their pain by reframing the issue in a more accurate light.

Just Talk

Most victims of abuse don't tell anyone. They suck it up and take it, even when help is just one conversation away. In order to help your child talk to you, get ahead of the game by promising your child that if they tell you about bullying, you will not run off to the school right away. Promise your child that you will make the decision together whether to tell the school or not.

Document what happened, especially who else witnessed the bullying, which is essential because many reports of bullying end up in a he-said/she-said situation, which favors the bully. Yet when two to four people are saying roughly the same thing, then you have some real information to present to the school. But above all this, please remember to tell your child that what is happening is wrong, that there is nothing wrong with your child, and you will always be by their side.

Notes

[1]Chuck Hustmyre and Jay Dixit, "How to Avoid Being a Victim: Tips on How Not to Be a Target of Crime," *Psychology Today* (January 2009), June 9, 2016, https://www.psychologytoday.com/us/articles/200901 /how-avoid-being-victim.

[2]Albert Mehrabian, "'Silent Messages'—A Wealth of Information About Nonverbal Communication (Body Language)," accessed May 20, 2018, http:// www.kaaj.com/psych/smorder.html.

[3]Amy Cuddy, "Your Body Language May Shape Who You Are," TED Global 2012, accessed December 20, 2017, https://www.ted.com/talks/amy_cuddy _your_body_language_shapes_who_you_are/transcript#t-687950.

[4]C. S. Lewis, *The Four Loves* (New York: Harcourt Brace, 1960), iBooks.

[5]Kirsten Fanning and M. David Piercey, "Internal Auditors' Use of Interpersonal Likability, Arguments, and Accounting Information in a Corporate Governance Setting," *Accounting, Organizations, and Society* 39, no 8, (2014): 575–89, https://doi.org/10.1016/j.aos.2014.07.002.

[6]Jack Zenger, "The Unlikeable Leader: Seven Ways to Improve Employee /Boss Relationships," *Forbes,* June 13, 2013, https://www.forbes.com/sites/ jackzenger/2013/06/13/the-unlikable-leader-7-ways-to-improve-employeeboss -relationships/#1a653ba21da6.

[7]Travis Bradberry, "Ten Habits of Unlikeable People," *Huffington Post,* March 26, 2017, https://www.huffingtonpost.com/entry/10-habits-of -unlikeable-people_us_58d2bbd7e4b002482d6e6d6b.

The Sermon That Stopped a School Massacre

When Richard Lemcke was a senior in high school, he did more than want to murder as many classmates as possible due to revenge against bullying. He planned his revenge, amassing a shotgun, a rifle, a handgun, and more than one thousand rounds of ammunition. He bought locks and chains so he could trap his prey in the gym. He hid his arsenal of vengeance throughout the school and set the date in his mind: February 5.

"If I was going to jail," he says, "I wasn't going to just kill one or even two. I created a list of fourteen girls and boys whom I wanted to kill. There were eight girls and six boys; but if I could find more, I wasn't going to hesitate to kill them, either."

His worst tormenters were often girls, who taunted him mostly through name-calling, the most common form of bullying. One attractive senior girl seemed to come out of nowhere. Without provocation or cause, she stared at Richard and put her finger in her mouth, imitating the act of gagging. Later, a girl in his class knocked his books out of his hands while bystanders laughed at him. Later that day, several classmates made the same disparaging gagging gesture.

He contemplated suicide that day. His rage grew and seemed to only cool as he planned and fantasized about his coming massacre. "Everything was set for the big day. All I had to do now was wait. I envisioned each person dead, on the floor begging for help and mercy."

But what Richard did not plan for was divine intervention.

Dave, a friend who stuck with him throughout his years of difficulty, invited Richard to church. "My first and only reaction was *Hell no!* The last thing I needed in my life was religion," he says. But Dave persisted, and Rich said yes—not because he really wanted to go but because Dave's attractive sister was going.

Rich says he hated church growing up, finding it "agonizingly boring, like going to a funeral." The sermons, he says, were simplistic and the songs went on forever. But there was something different about this gathering and this pastor. "I felt as though a new world had opened up to me—everything that was happening around me went against what I had been taught about church, like raising your hands and praising God out loud."

Then an older, pudgy man took the stage and asked, "Do you like the direction your life is going? If you were to die tonight, would you go to heaven?" Rich's thoughts took wild swings. "One minute, I'd think this whole thing was a hoax. Then the next minute, I had a sense of complete peace. It was as though his sermon had been aimed directly at me."

Rich was one of the first people to say yes to the alter call at the end of the sermon. He spoke with counselors and asked many questions regarding forgiveness. With tears running down his face, he recited the Sinner's Prayer and begged God for his forgiveness and mercy. His countenance changed within minutes. Dave later told him that he noticed his eyes change from "dark as death" to being "bright blue and full of life."

With forgiveness in his heart and hope for a brighter future in his soul, Rich knew that he had to somehow remove the weapons he'd hid throughout the school. He found an unlocked door at the school, and after tense moments that included a run in with one of his bullies as well as being followed by a police officer, he succeeded.

His acceptance of God's love and forgiveness didn't stop the bullying. "But instead of getting mad, I simply forgave them in my heart, though I struggled to forgive all my classmates." His grade point average went from a 2.3 to nearly a 3.4.

By accepting Jesus as his Lord and Savior, Rich Lemcke received divine help in draining the lake of rage within him. He gained greater inspiration, love, and wisdom to better navigate the storms of life. At the same time, Rich still acknowledges the real effects of bullying—even after a conversion experience. Contrary to some of the optimistic but erroneous testimonies that we hear in church, the multifaceted results of sustained abuse don't disappear, and they rarely "make us stronger."

Rich wants bullies, bystanders, and others to know that the emotional scars from bullying still linger. "Even after thirty years, I get tears in my eyes when I think back to the mental torture, humiliation, and rejection I endured." Since most of his bullies were women, he says he has "difficulty trusting them, and [has] an even harder time being around them. I'm constantly afraid that they will betray me, tease me, or say untruthful things about me. I will never have the confidence I should have around women as a result of being bullied."

Perhaps the most tragic part of his story, he says, was bystander apathy. Repeating the dismay of so many other serial targets, he says for "bullying to go away, someone has to make a stand. This may mean calling the police, but by all means, don't just ignore it! To my coach, don't tell me or others to 'just grow up' while we get our heads smashed into lockers! Have the empathy and courage to say 'Enough!' You could have protected me."

To his teachers, he says, "You refused to address the issues in class. I asked to be moved to a different seat, and you said no. You didn't have time for me after class. You saw them trip me and did nothing. Gum was put in my hair, and you still did nothing. I begged for help."

To a lifelong friend of his parents, he says, "You watched me grow up and spent countless hours with my parents. Why did you allow the cheerleaders to mock me and call me names during football games? Why didn't you at least tell my parents? Were you afraid of your precious reputation? I was hurting, and you ignored my pain. Afterward, you didn't even counsel me while I was in tears."

To his fellow targets who, like him, have thought about hurting themselves and harming others, he says the good news is that you can leave your dark place of torment. "You can experience joy despite the onslaught of bullying. You can be a victor instead of being a victim. Let me introduce you to my best friend, who knows your pain, who knows your name, and who cares about you more than anyone ever will. He's the same friend who took me out of darkness. His name is Jesus Christ. Allow him to come into your heart. Let him transform you and give you the strength and hope that you so desperately seek."

CHAPTER NINE

Misuse of Scripture Enables Bullying

Jesus's teaching "Judge not" means "Do not condemn." It does not mean "Don't try to discern the difference between right and wrong." —Glen Stassen and David Gushee

MUST WE ALWAYS LOVE OUR ENEMIES? MUST WE ALWAYS FORGIVE THEM? IS IT REALLY A SIN TO BE ANGRY WITH those who bully and abuse you? The misuse and misapplication of Scriptures addressing these issues has led to more anguish and pain than we can imagine. In this chapter, we'll address three larger philosophical and spiritual obstacles that many targets face due to the misuse of Scripture that can unintentionally enable bullying. They are the combustible topic of anger, the multifaceted process of forgiveness, and our struggle to properly handle an enemy.

Life on Fire

Christians cast a suspicious eye on anger—and for good reason. It can be a consuming fire where even one act of unrestrained anger can haunt a person for a lifetime. Though the apostle Paul tells us that a person can feel anger, and even must feel anger, and still not sin (Eph. 4:26), we find this consumptive emotion so bothersome and off-putting that we've decided as a whole to stay far away from it. Nothing good can come from anger, we've concluded.

This part of our "nice church" script has made life unintentionally harder for targets of abuse. For reasons explained earlier, we are more likely to lecture an abused person for expressing anger than we are to admonish her bully for being cruel or even wicked. This miscarriage of fairness leaves the impression on the abused that the problem begins and ends with them. We do so because as a grace-lensed people, we are quick (and sometimes too quick) to point out ungracious responses. We also respond this way because we want to see kindness, mercy, and compassion win. But we can be negligent in how we try to shepherd this important task. So negligent that we actually ruin a victim's chances of winning—in part because we rush the process, like taking a cake out of the oven before it has time to bake all the way through. To make matters more difficult, we sometimes don't see the deeper meaning of what Jesus has told us in key passages that come up regularly when we talk about bullying. We sometimes find ourselves in the middle of a double-misconception: what Jesus is really talking about, and what serial bullying is really about.

One of those key passages has to do with anger, which we tell targets to discard right away. Targets as young as eight are told, "But I tell you that anyone who is angry with a brother or sister will be subject to judgment" (Matt. 5:22 NIV). Some versions of this verse include the phrase "nurses anger" toward a brother or sister "without good cause." Others say, "brought to judgment" instead of subject to judgment. However, it's important to point out that nursing anger is very different from feeling anger. Nursing anger means to keep it alive, to give it harbor, and to even cherish it, which can feel pleasurable. *Feeling* anger due to abuse is normal;

nursing anger can lead to resentment, bitterness, and thoughts and actions of revenge, harming both the target and the bully.

To show our unacknowledged prejudice against the abused, let me tell you about a meeting I had at a Christian school. The target and the bully, both in middle school, were brought into the principal's office in an attempt to resolve the problem. The principal read the first part of Matt. 5:22 to the target, yet did not read the very next sentence to the bully, which reads, "If he abuses his brother he must answer for it to the court; if he sneers at him he will have to answer for it in the fires of hell" (Matt. 5:22 NEB).

Chances are you are not as familiar with this second part of this verse because it's rarely, if ever, highlighted in sermons. By now, I hope you see that this isn't an accident within the church culture where we are more concerned about expressions of anger that make us uncomfortable than we are with acts of abuse. We often care more about our own comfort than we do about justice.

It's not that the bully got away without strong words in that meeting. But he did escape biblical admonition, unlike the target. I've seen this happen other times as well. I think another reason we are so quick to admonish the abused is because they are usually nicer, so they are prone to take it. We also fear bullies and their families because we fear what they will do to us, making us peace-fakers, not peacemakers.

In order to make sense of *what* Jesus is saying, we have to be clear on *who* he's talking to, and *what* he's talking about. Here in Matthew 5, we can assume he's still talking to his disciples, not confused and abused eight-year-old boys and girls being harmed daily at school. We also need to keep in mind *how* he spoke. He was often a hurricane of change, sometimes speaking in ways to jolt his audience in order to help them see through the religious and cultural wool pulled over their eyes, perhaps the hardest kind to penetrate. So, he taught with vivid juxtapositions in order to bring clarity to higher truths that his audience could understand and remember. But he didn't speak to every aspect of human ignorance, sin, or evil. Jesus spoke much more like a pithy and terse dictionary than a multivolume encyclopedia.

But *what* is he talking about? Jesus is confronting the common way of thinking that says the line of morality is drawn by what is legal and illegal. This is deduced earlier in the same passage where he says, "You have heard that it was said to an older generation, 'Do not murder,' and 'whoever murders will be subjected to judgment'" (Matt. 5:21). Jesus is confronting this misconception head on with powerful imagery and examples. If we think this is a problem of the past, think again. You have probably scratched your head like I have when you hear about a pastor who is let go by a church for immoral behavior, yet people defend the pastor by saying, "He didn't do anything illegal." Yet their excuse of the pastor's sin is exactly what Jesus is speaking against. As usual, Jesus is going after the heart—what we cherish and value, and what motivates us to action. He's telling us that our bar for morality should be much higher than just the law—if you're going to be his disciple and want to please God. He's telling us that not only is murder wrong, but so is harboring anger toward another that could lead to murder—a soul problem no court can fix.

Forgive Your Bullies

Another area where our grace-tinted lenses can betray us is in the realm of relational forgiveness, which can unintentionally leave our abused children more susceptible to ongoing bullying. We may possess loads of zeal when it comes to forgiveness, but we can be deficient in our knowledge of how to create it (Rom. 10:2).

In *Extraordinary Evil: A Short Walk to Genocide,* Barbara Coloroso, a former Franciscan nun, connects the scourge of bullying to the evil of genocide. Toward the end, she reveals a searing example of just how poorly some people of faith can handle the topic of forgiveness:

> For too long we have been taught that we must forgive those who have harmed us—especially when they ask for forgiveness. It doesn't seem to matter whether they are sincere or what their motives are: whether they are asking for forgiveness to be relieved of their own guilt, or to avoid a longer prison sentence. . . . In April 2004, at a ceremony in Kigali, Rwanda, marking the ten-year anniversary of the genocide, one speaker assured all those who had asked for forgiveness for their crimes in the genocide that they would be forgiven and would "sit at the right hand of God." Those who refused to forgive the *genocidaires* for killing their children in front of them, butchering their kin, for hunting them like animals, would find themselves "burning in Hell" for refusing to forgive—one more burden on those already overburdened with nightmares, sorrow, poverty, and a loss that cannot be compensated.[1]

I first met Mike Conley in New York when I was speaking at the school associated with the church where he was pastor. I had no idea that my experience with bullying would force him to confront his own past abuse and struggles with forgiveness.

His bullying began in middle school at the hands of a group of boys who bullied him through thuggish insults, intimidation, shoving that progressed into tripping, and throwing his books and papers across the room. But as is often the case, the bullying escalated. "When no one in authority was looking, which was rare, they cornered me, picked me up, and shoved me into a locker and slammed the door. Walking away hysterical at their accomplishment, I was left inside the locker. It was dark and the small space pressed in hard on all sides. Humiliation, physical pain, and fear of the consequences of missing my next class filled my racing mind. I had no idea when they would come back." When they did come back, the lead bully, who Mike calls the "Big One," lifted him off the ground by the shirt and called him a "worthless piece of [expletive]." He let go of Mike only to punch him. "I fell backward to the floor in humiliation. They threatened me with more abuse as I limped away in shock and gathered my composure enough to hurry to my class. "What had I done to become the object of this?" he thought to himself.

Showers were mandatory after gym class, a ritual of embarrassment and humiliation for many targets. And they were largely unsupervised, and a haven for bullies. He would shower as quickly as he could and get out of that place that he described as his "own personal concentration camp." But when he went to get his towel off the hook, it was missing. His bullies, who he calls "The Ones," had taken it. They cornered him and called him derogatory names. They told Mike that more abuse was coming.

They memorized his class schedule so they could torment him even more. The Big One would say repeatedly when he walked by, "You can run, but you can't hide. Tic-Toc, Tic-Toc . . ." Time, he wanted Mike to know, was on their side.

Mike dreaded going to middle school and, like so many other targets, came up with pseudo-physical reasons not to go to school. Sunday evenings were the worst for him because that's when he began to ruminate about his coming misery. "One would think that I would have shared this panic and dread with my family, or the school leaders, but in my family culture, stoicism and perseverance and duty were held in such high value, I just couldn't bring myself to tell anyone. I knew what their response would be, 'Just give it right back to them,' and 'Buck up and be a man.' I was eleven years old. I did talk to God. He was the only one I ever shared my abuses with. Mainly, my prayers were pleads for help and deliverance from what was happening. It helped to talk about it with God; but unfortunately, things went from bad to worse."

(Trigger warning—Mike's story gets graphic.) His locker room was empty after gym class. "One of them barred the door and turned out the lights. I went into a panic and ran into the trainer's room. It was windowless with a flat table, which I hid behind. My heart began to race, while the rest of me was frozen still in hopes that they wouldn't find me there in the dark. I was discovered. They encircled me and spewed profane insults and said I deserved to be punished. They picked me up like one would pick up a baby. More humiliation." Mike tried to struggle free, but was repeatedly punched in the gut and face, which subdued him. "They held me down on the metal table. It was ice cold. They ripped down my pants. Taking a nearby broom handle, they dipped the tip in Atom Balm, the gel-like liniment used by athletes to apply to injured areas. It was designed to burn to disguise the pain. I will never forget that wintergreen-menthol smell. The lesser ones held my legs spread eagle while the Big One shoved it inside me, telling me I was a 'stinking whore,' and that I enjoyed it. Laughing, they pulled out the handle and threw the broom in the corner, unbarred the door, and left. Try as I might to clean off the Atom Balm from myself, the burning stayed for hours, and the effects forever."

Mike prayed they would get caught, that "they would get hit by a truck or anything to get me out of this hell that I was caught in. You would think I might give up praying, but I still did, hoping for deliverance, for an advocate, a protector."

He had a paper route after school, which he really enjoyed. It helped Mike deal with some of the emotional trauma, because the "cadence of plodding for miles every afternoon allowed me to lapse into a sort of hypnotic zone. It also was somewhat of a safe zone, away from school." Then his bullies did what Michael Corleone from *The Godfather* warned, "When they come, they come at what you love." They stalked him and would randomly show up along his route to say "Tic-Toc" as he rode by.

One nondescript afternoon, he rounded a corner on his route with no homes or traffic. Just an abandoned weathered old barn that sat close to the street. As he rode by, the bullies grabbed him and brought him inside. The leader slammed him to the ground and put a rolled up bandana in his mouth to stop his cries for help from being heard, and to make it easier to throw him around by his head and neck. He told me his story:

> They shouted at me to take off my jeans. And then it began. The Big One started it. I was gang raped by all of them. Five times. My face was rhythmically slammed into the floor. The pain was excruciating and like shards of broken glass. Near the end, I lost consciousness, at least on some level. I came to enough to find myself half naked, bleeding, and broken. Crawling to search for my jeans to cover myself, I found them thrown in the corner. I managed to slip them on and limp my way back home as the light went out in the sky and in my soul.
>
> I no longer could depend on the abuse staying within the borders of school. They had breached the gap, and now I was playing a game of hide and seek, but there was no "safe." I was raped again the same way six months later in a wooded area at the opposite end of my route. But the anticipation that I felt every day, that it could happen again any day, damaged my mind. I became highly anxious and hypervigilant to the point of paranoia, and I was prone to panic attacks. My grades suffered; I couldn't sleep. And believe it or not, I still

prayed. Sometimes asking why, and always pleading for help.

My prayers were finally answered, and help did finally come in the form of the Big One moving away. This event caused his minions to drop their pattern of abuse. They had lost their kingpin, and they lost the guts or the inspiration, and the abuse stopped. Relief like I can't explain flooded through me, and life became so much better. Outside I was "better," but the feeling of "safe" didn't return. I was still filled with fear whenever I saw one of them while they acted as though the abuse had never happened. I wanted a feeling of protection so desperately.

My friend Mike would later embark on a series of homosexual relationships, where he says he sunk into promiscuity to mask and subdue his pain.

This former pastor says he has not forgiven those five boys. "They still remain faceless in my memory. I especially have not forgiven the leader, though I feel some of the other bullies were his victims in some way as well."

He has had no contact with any of these individuals for more than forty years, "yet they live on inside my inner world. I am continuing to seek to divest them of their power to run rogue through my mind and life by putting the traumatic events into a context that affirms my pain, and diminishes their power to intimidate and torment me on an everyday basis."

"I am on what feels like a journey of microns," he says.

I cannot shake the realization that some reading this are more concerned with Mike's un-forgiveness than with the horrors that produces it. We behave as if the word *forgiveness* appears in the Bible 130 times and the word *justice* just thirteen, not the other way around. Some are more likely to admonish Mike than the Big One. Contrary to the convenient myth, we see in Mike's story how bullying does not benefit many later in life. He is fifty-seven, and the paint on his house of horror hasn't dried. It probably never will.

We forgive because it can foster genuine reconciliation and peace in our home, church, school, and community. And we forgive for our own best interest since un-forgiveness, so prone to gnawing the dry bones of resentment, bitterness, and hatred, can be a soul poison. This is probably at least one reason why Jesus commands us to forgive others. We forgive not to change the oppressor, but to change ourselves as a form of self-defense and self-care.

Yet having been a bully magnet for part of my life, I know how foolish and dangerous it is to equate forgiveness with reconciliation. For true reconciliation to form, there has to be a leaning in from *both* parties, which is rare when dealing with serial bullies while they still sit in seats of power. What almost always creates a leaning in from serial bullies is some form of injury to their health, income, or reputation. This injury may foster needed humility, which almost always precedes deeper spiritual change and maturity. We find this truth many times in the Bible, especially in 2 Chronicles 7:14: "If my people, who are called by my name, will humble themselves and pray and seek my face and turn from their wicked ways, then I will hear from heaven, and I will forgive their sin." Here we see the connection between wickedness and lack of humility. Through humility, we find a powerful antidote to wickedness.

Genocide survivor Lawrence Martin Jenco, in *Bound to Forgive,* gives this eloquent insight when it comes to the personal power of forgiveness: "I forgive, but I remember. I do not forget the pain, the loneliness, the ache, the terrible injustice. But I do not remember it to inflict guilt or some future retribution. Having forgiven, I am liberated. I need no longer be determined by the past. I move into the future free to imagine new possibilities."[2]

During my work with the Baltimore Ravens, I discovered pretty quickly how important forgiveness is in the hearts and souls of pro-football players. That's because there's something fundamentally wrong with football culture. Of all the complaints we receive about a sports program that includes both players and coaches, more than 90 percent are about football. Football culture promotes bullying, and the Ravens are wise and recognize it.[3] They know how past acts of bullying can make even a professional player uncoachable. These players, even when they hear helpful and constructive feedback about their play, mistake it for the horrendous treatment of their former bully coaches. The anger and even hatred they felt afterward fueled them through high school and college football, but becomes a brake in the pros, spinning them out of control, leaving them (and their coaches) frustrated and unable to evolve.

I brought with me to training camp, almost as an afterthought, multiple copies of a powerful little booklet, *How Do I Forgive?* by Everett Worthington Jr. I recommend it to targets of bullying all the time, and figured the players would appreciate not just its message, but how quick it would be to read given their very busy schedules. They were gone within a minute. Players asked for two of them so they could give one to their buddy.

In it, Worthington cuts through a lot of the smog that can exist within faith communities about the very serious business of forgiveness. One insight that's essential for targets is Worthington's example of how forgiveness exists in two flavors: Decisional Forgiveness, which is how you would intend to act or would act if you had the chance; and Emotional Forgiveness, where we replace negative feelings toward the bully with positive feelings. So, for example, a target's feeling of resentment might be replaced with feelings of compassion. He points out that emotional forgiveness is stronger, but it's not required to forgive, and he says God doesn't require it either.

He highlights another essential point: forgiveness doesn't require reconciliation. Sometimes it's dangerous to reconcile with another person since doing so can easily open the target's life to more pain and suffering. It's surprising how many times I need to point this out to parents of targets.

I sometimes end my presentation at the Ravens with a quote from Martin Luther King Jr.: "Forgiveness is not an occasional act; it is a constant attitude." King said that we should best view forgiveness as a process, and I have found in my work with targets that this is some of the best advice they can receive. Because sometimes, they just can't bring themselves to do it. And if we leave them with a one-time act as their only option, they are left hopeless. Framing forgiveness in terms of a process is not only more accurate; it's more loving. At the same time, having worked with many targets, I believe one-time forgiveness is possible. Some people have this unique capacity. And I also believe that such an act can be a gift from God.

King recommended meditative prayer, where the target recounts the offense and at the same time invites Jesus's thoughts, words, actions, and love into the drama, reframing (eventually) the incident and cooling raw emotions. To aid this journey, he said, "There is some good in the worst of us and some evil in the best of us. Whenever we discover this, we are less prone to hate our enemies."

My progress through the process of forgiveness toward my bullies has been fostered by the following insight: For whom and what are you willing to suffer? I mention this because it's only human to recount those bullying events that cause so much pain years later. It's common, though not beneficial, to ruminate upon them. I did this for decades, and I suffered. But then, when I gained this insight, I was able to break the cycle of rumination through the truth that my former bullies are not worthy of my suffering. But bullied children are. I continue to sacrifice for them. Who in your life is worthy of your suffering and sacrifice? Spend your thoughts and actions on them, not your bullies.

Another practice that helped me ward off resentment from past bullying is to be present in each moment. This sounds like a no-brainer, but it wasn't at first. Too often, memories of past abuse stole present happiness, pleasure, and contentment. The truth of a great sermon, laughter among friends, an endearing comment from one of my children—I allowed these and countless other blessings to be stolen from me because my mind was set upon the past. I am still learning to stop during these moments of rumination and focus on what is in front of me right now. It can be something simple, like looking out a window at a pine tree and really experiencing it. During these moments and through this practice, I am more open to truth, goodness, and beauty.

Pray for Your Enemies

Our word for prayer comes from the same root as the word *precarious,* which is a great word to describe the theater of bullying. The admonishments to pray for and love our enemies and to forgive those who sin against us distinguish Christianity from other expressions of faith. But one of the more troubling aspects of Jesus's commandment is that he doesn't tell us *how* to pray for our enemies. As grace-inspired and love-infused people, we can assume that we should pray for the well-being of the bully.

So, when I pray for the bullies who torment the targets who ask us for help, I pray for what they need in order to become more loving and less abusive people. What most bullies need in order to be more loving is humility, an antidote to their arrogance. So I encourage targets and their families to pray for humility for their bully as well. But I caution them not to try to figure out how God delivers the humility, which can be a real hang-up for targets and their families. I encourage them to leave that up to God and to keep their minds on more important matters, such as their own wellness—because in praying for our enemies, we are praying for ourselves as well. We pray for an increase in our own strength, wisdom, courage, and hope. We pray that God will help us let go of the pain we feel and deliver us from the lies that evil has told us. I have said these prayers myself many times. They aren't magic, but they are remarkable because they remind me of God's love for me. They relax me. On the other side of them, my fears are calmed, and I become a more loving person. My bullies grow strangely dim, as well. It's not that they aren't alive anymore. But the pall that they can still throw upon me many years later dissipates. Prayer dismantles fear when said within God's love for us. I have even found myself chuckling after these prayers because I realize again how little power many of my bullies actually had. I also know that if we don't pray for the well-being of our bully, we will curse our bully; and in cursing them, we poison ourselves. I have done this many times as well. I prefer the chuckles.

Who and What Is an Enemy?

The word *enemy* appears in the Bible 112 times. Its most famous usage is also one of the most quoted in the theater of bullying: "You have heard that it was said, 'Love your neighbor' and 'hate your enemy.' But I say to you, love your enemy and pray for those who persecute you" (Matt. 5:43–44). Paul fortifies Jesus's words when he wrote, "If your enemy is hungry, feed him; if he is thirsty, give him a drink; for in doing this you will be heaping burning coals on his head" (Rom. 12:20).

Even an acute bully constitutes an enemy. That's the easy part to figure out. The real problem we have is knowing how a target of intentional and undeserved abuse should treat her enemy. One way to answer this question in light of Scripture is to insert the name of a specific form of abuse into these powerful Scriptures:

"If your rapist is hungry, feed him; if your rapist is thirsty, give him something to drink."

"Love the person who sexually assaults you, psychologically destroys you, and sold you into sex trafficking at age of twelve."

Is this really what God requires?

Did Jesus really mean the following?

"Do not resist the person who rapes you. If your rapist slaps you on the cheek, don't resist him; let him keep slapping you."

"If your rapist wants your blouse, give him your pants as well."

"Do not resist the man in authority. If your rapist rapes you once, let him rape you twice."

Bullies always assault our honor and sometimes our possessions, but they do more than that. They, like rapists, assault our value, reputation, self-worth, dignity, and self-respect. They assault our belief in a loving and merciful God. Their assault goes so deep into the human soul that targets are two to nine times more likely to consider suicide, with suicide being now the second leading cause of death among youth. Rape victims are four times more likely to consider suicide.

All but the most ignorant and cold-hearted among us believe there are reasonable exceptions to what Jesus said about enemies—if those enemies are adults. But many do not when it comes to the leading form of child abuse in the nation.

My purpose here is to get us to add bullied children to this list of exceptions, the way we currently add victims of rape, sex trafficking, domestic abuse, stalking, harassment, and related criminal behavior. Because bullies don't hurt; they harm. Bullies don't bother; they destroy. Bullies don't misunderstand; they malign. They don't miscommunicate; they intentionally murder the spirit of another. Many would be arrested if they did to an adult what they do to other children.

Notes

[1] Coloroso, *Extraordinary Evil*, 205–6.

[2] Coloroso, *Extraordinary Evil*, 204.

[3] For more proof, read the illuminating Ted Wells Report (February 14, 2014) about bullying within the Miami Dolphins, which led to the firing of coach Jim Turner and trainer Kevin O'Neill. See Theodore V. Wells Jr., Brad S. Karp, Bruce Birenboim, and David W. Brown, "Report to the National Football League Concerning Issues of Workplace Conduct at the Miami Dolphins," February 14, 2014, http://63bba9dfdf9675bf3f10-68be460ce43dd2a60dd64ca 5eca4ae1d.r37.cf1.rackcdn.com/PaulWeissReport.pdf.

Bullied before He Was Crucified

Crucifixion was created to make the demonic real in the lives of the crucified, their loved ones, and those passing by. It was designed to terrorize and dissuade witnesses from committing the same offense against the authority of the state. It is from this horrific form of capital punishment that we get today's word "excruciating," which means, "out of crucifying."

This gruesome form of torture was fashioned to make its victim believe that they were forsaken well before they died. To make them, like Job, wish they had never been born. Its creators labored to destroy a victim's soul before their body extinguished.

I've had one night terror as an adult (at least that's what I call it). It was strange because it hit me during a good stretch in my life. Everything that was important to me was going well, so I had no major worries or anxiety weighing me down.

Yet I awoke one summer night from a kind of video clip of hell. I will never be able to fully describe how it felt. The best I can say is that the essential me, my soul, was untethered from an animating force, energy, or power that had been previously given to me.

But it was worse than that. Because as I was untethered and separated from this Force, I also lost all form and structure. I literally thrashed and gnashed my teeth. I was becoming no one, nowhere. I was losing existence and had no means of getting it back.

I was more than becoming dismantled; for a moment, I felt forsaken, separated from God's animating love, and I was terrified. And when I awoke, gulping air, and yelled, "Oh my God!" I meant it in the rescuing sense. I dreamt a nightmare, Jesus lived one.

The Romans tailored crucifixion so that it stole a person's past, present, and future by fragmenting his mind and stealing his very identity and separating him from the animating force of life. And this primitive instrument of torture included the cruelest traits of bullying: superior power, humiliation, isolation, terror, sadism, scorn, hubris, mockery, betrayal, treachery, the public display of pain and anguish, and threat of further abuse if anyone else got out of line. The way Jesus refused the myrrh offered him by a lone sympathetic guard to lessen his misery is the most forgotten miracle.

Jesus was bullied before he was murdered.

Because he endured relentless bullying, he knows our exact pain as targets. He felt what all targets feel. Yet with cosmic irony, the bullying he endured has given countless others the inspiration, courage, and strength to topple countless bullies and every form of injustice. Through him being bullied, we are freed from bullying.

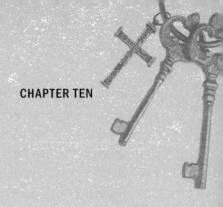

CHAPTER TEN

From Witness to Protector

And now that they'd protected me, I was different to them. It was like I was one of them. They all called me "little dude" now—even the jocks. –August Pullman, *Wonder*

IN 2003, A GERMAN TELEVISION STATION ASKED GERMANS AGED EIGHTEEN TO FORTY WHO IS THE GREATEST GERMAN of all time. They named Sophia Scholl and her brother Hans before Bach and even Einstein. They were the heart, mind, and courage behind the White Rose Resistance in Nazi Germany, which, through a series of pamphlets, encouraged Germans to oppose the Nazi government. While distributing the sixth pamphlet, they were discovered by a guard, arrested, and soon beheaded.

Sophia and Hans came in fourth in the poll. Yet here's the telling part when it comes to bullying and youth today: if the votes of only the young viewers were counted, she and her brother would have been first. A German magazine for women voted Scholl "the greatest woman of the twentieth century."

Yet many people outside of Germany have never even heard about this woman of deep Christian faith and fiery spirit, a trait we unfortunately don't associate with deep faith. We know about Bach, who swells our hearts, and Einstein, who blows our minds. But it's Scholl who attracts like a magnet our third fundamental human capacity as beings made in the image of God, a capacity that is the missing piece in our anti-bullying puzzle. She speaks to our courage—and with it our heroic imagination, a trait that burns within our youth, often more than in adults. It's the key to liberating millions of targets of bullying each year, because in order to diminish bullying, we must enlist the bystander since targets are unlikely to provide useful resistance on their own. They need others to help them. But youth bystanders need adults to help them take what's in their noble imagination and commit acts of tangible courage and strength and, with both, love.

Our *thumos* is home to courage and strength, which are nearly synonymous in the Bible. It's the seat of willpower and pugnacity, essential characteristics we must possess if we're serious about justice, righteousness, and a life well-lived. It's where we get today's word for Thermos, a container of inner heat, our inner-Popeye. It's where indignation, a mature expression of anger and grief, is birthed and nurtured, which leads us to act heroically upon what grieves us to the glory of God and the benefit of his beloved creation.

And what's fascinating about this fundamental human capacity is that the Bible actually commands us to love God and our neighbor through our thumotic courage and strength. In Mark 12:28–31, Jesus responds to the question from a lawyer with the most important of all commandments. Jesus says, "Love the Lord your God with all your heart, with all your soul, with all your mind, and with all your *strength*" (emphasis mine). And the second is to "Love your neighbor as yourself" through these same abilities and capacities. We're familiar with expressing love through our emotions, such as affection, and through our minds, such as sharing life-giving wisdom with others. But through our strength and capacity for courage? Chances are you've read this passage many times, but this is the first time you've really seen it. That's because sometimes when we handle sacred texts too many times, we fail to see what's really there. God has been telling us something very important about courage for a very long time. We haven't been listening, or acting, like we should.

He's been telling us something important about anger, as well, because anger is also required to transform bystanders into righteous Protectors.

Timothy Keller, in a sermon entitled "Forgiving and Forgiven" (based on Eph. 4:25–32), says some of us are sinning because we aren't angry enough at what angers God. Although Paul tells us to not sin in our anger, he also tells us to be angry. "Paul says 'Be angry,' it's imperative, it's a command. 'Be angry,' must mean that suppression or denial of anger is wrong," Keller says. Sometimes, when we're not angry, he says, "you are wrong." No emotion in and of itself is a sin. What happens, he says, is that they go bad because they are tainted by sin, like fruit that goes rancid.

Keller reminds us that God hates evil, and Jesus expressed anger, specifically indignation, which is "a zeal to see justice done." He cites a specific example of indignation Jesus shows toward the Pharisees in Mark 3, a story commonly known as "The Man with a Withered Hand." This man with the deformed hand was in the congregation in the synagogue on the Sabbath, and the Pharisees watched Jesus to see if he would break the Sabbath in order to heal the man, thereby "bringing a charge" against Jesus for violating the Sabbath (Mark 3:3).

Jesus then commits a behavior that is deemed by some as so unchristian that it could get you removed as a church leader. He looked at the Pharisees with indignation in his eyes and sorrow for their obstinate stupidity (Mark 3:5). "Why?" asks Keller.

> Anger is aroused in the defense of something good and released against something evil. If you see something threatened that is wonderful and good, and you don't get angry, you are not a good person. If you see some-one being oppressed, if you see someone being used, if you see justice being trampled on, and you don't get angry, you are not like God.[1]

In essence, the more holy you become, Keller says, the more angry you're going to get when you witness injustice and oppression.

Bullied children are oppressed.

Does this bolder orientation toward life that's intrinsic to *shalom* describe the Christians you know? Does it describe three of them? Even one? I know a church-going man who is respon-sible for the anti-bullying efforts within a school district. I have never heard him get angry about the bullying he is expected to diminish, reminding me of that disturbing observation from C. S. Lewis: "If the parents in each generation always or often knew what really goes on at their sons' schools, the history of education would be very different."[2] The only time I have ever heard him get angry is when his early retirement was threatened.

We humans are similar to engines, which need three sub-stances to create propulsion: air, fuel, and spark. For action to take place on behalf of justice in the theater of bullying, three sub-stances are needed as well: what our minds know, what our hearts feel, and what our thumotic courage—fueled by indignation—propels us to do. Indignation is part of the engine of change for the benefit of others and for our own spiritual ripening. I launched The Protectors nearly fifteen years ago because I felt more than sorrow for targets. I was angry and indignant at what I saw around me, causing me to get off my blessed assurance and get onto the messy, difficult, but also rewarding playing field of life.

Our *thumos* is where our heart and mind converge, argue, contend with fear, consider risks, move forward, or succumb to the sin of cowardice, reminding me of what Emerson wrote: "God will not have His work manifest by cowards." It's through faith and courage that action is created—the kind of action Jesus's half-brother, blunt James, writes about. And not just his most famous truth: "Faith by itself, if it is not accompanied by action, is dead" (James 2:17 NIV). At the very beginning of his pithy letter about practical religion, he writes about how the testing of one's faith brings fortitude, a fruit and expression of courage, and if this fortitude is brought to maturity, it leads to a balanced character that falls short of nothing (James 1:3–4). Another word for balanced character is integrity. Faith is not enough to have integrity, he tells us. Courage is in the mix as well.

But our courage is under assault because if this portion of our spiritual grid is damaged or removed, we have a religion without action, exactly what the enemy of our soul wants. Sentiment but not righteousness. Desire but not resolve. We have belief, but we don't have faith, which compels us to act for and against what God is for and against. Throw the spiritual bit of courage and strength from our mouth and we are free to consume but not produce, take without giving. We are free to be spectators instead of doers. Without courage in our spiritual mix, we are finally free to be lazy, or lazier than we already are. Courage is a vegetable of our faith, which at first isn't pleasing or appealing, but without which we are undernourished. Courage is our spiritual protein that builds strong spiritual muscles.

But there is a real problem with courage as it relates to moral and spiritual development. Studies also tell us that courage grows stronger with age. So how can we speed up courage development across the country and in our schools in order to transform bystanders into Protectors—those who stand up for the bullied but don't become bullies themselves? It's a challenge, yet we've been doing it for years.

A Script to Follow

I met an American veteran who was ambushed as he commanded a group of men in Vietnam. They were working their way up the face of a hill in the evening when the hounds of war descended upon them through rifle and machine-gun fire. The forest exploded, and they were about to be massacred.

"What did you do?" I asked.

"We pushed through the ambush. Stay put and you die," he said.

Through the ambush?! Are you kidding! I thought to myself. I would hide behind a rock, or tree. I'd retreat. There is no way I would continue up that mountain—but that's because they had something I don't.

They pushed through the ambush not because they possessed super-human courage, but because they were given a kind of nutrient that grew their courage. They were given a script to follow ahead of time, and they practiced it over and over until it became second nature.

Like a commercial pilot when an engine blows up, they had a game plan to follow, they practiced that game plan, and they had trust and faith in the game plan. To bring God's love, light, and justice into the theater of bullying, we must supply bystanders with the very same thing.

Our children will heroically stand up to bullying if we empower them with the tools they need to be redemptive forces of good and to wage decisive peace in our schools and communities. This is one reason why our curriculum includes scenarios for each student to role-play. They learn what it's like to be a target, a bully, and most importantly, a Protector. They are given the words to say and are shown the right way to say them. And the results are amazing. One University of Oregon study shows that if only one person, and they don't have to be popular or even large in size, uses assertive but nonviolent words when they witness bullying, such as "Stop" or "Leave her alone," the incident of bullying can end 58 percent of the time and within six to eight seconds.

This makes me think of Melody.

Her fifth-grade teacher, Diane Alosi, at Silverdale Baptist Academy in Chattanooga, Tennessee, wrote us a letter telling us what Melody did, and how other students can do it too.

> I love teaching this material because it's exciting to see my students understand the power and responsibility they have to stand up for themselves and others. One of my students, Melody, heard a student bullying another student. Melody, a very small child, walked up and spoke boldly, using words straight from the Protectors Program. When Melody shared this with our class, her classmates spontaneously, without my direction, stood up and applauded her. Melody and the former bully are now friends and together they help defend other class-mates! This is just one example of how this program empowers students to do the right thing.

Melody completed The Protectors curriculum, which at the end has a *Courage & Character Commitment* that each student can take or not take. She took it. It includes committing to being a Protector of others, which includes reporting to authority acts of bullying as well as direct intervention. It also includes being helpful to people who are different than you, and to report if someone plans to bring a weapon to school. Melody said three words any child can say, "Leave her alone." They are the exact three words Jesus said when protecting Mary against one of the disciples (Mark 14:6). Melody stood up to bullying in part because her school had given her a script to follow, which she practiced. And Melody stood up to bullying because standing up to bullying was a family value. Her parents expected her to stand against bullying when it was within her power to act.

"Only the Gods Are Courageous in Isolation"

Solomon Asch, along with Stanley Milgram (who was a protégé of Asch), Phillip Zimbardo, and others, was a pioneer in the world of social psychology.[3] His most famous experiment, which would later be known as the Asch Conformity Experiment, shows us just how hard it is to stand against negative peer pressure on our own, and how much easier it is when we have someone standing by our side.

In this experiment, which has been replicated and confirmed many times since it was originally conducted in the 1950s, eight college students were asked to perform a simple task. Each student viewed a card with a single line on it, and then was given another card that had a set of lines labeled A, B, and C. One of the lines was the same length as the line on the first card. The other two were clearly longer or shorter. Participants were asked which line from the second group of lines matched the first line. In reality, seven of the eight students were actors who were told what answers to give.

During the first two go-arounds, the actors were instructed to give the right answer. But on the third go around, the actors were told to give the same wrong answer. Asch wanted to find out what the only non-actor would do. Would the subject give a deliberately wrong answer in order to fit in, or would he stand against the group and do the right thing, even though it was uncomfortable?

Asch found that when the subject stood alone, only about 37 percent gave the right answer. But when Asch instructed one of the seven actors to give the right answer before the subject could respond, yielding to negative peer pressure dropped to just 5 percent. When the subject had a confederate, he was far more courageous.

We call this the Power of Two, and we see it in other aspects of life as well. Jesus sent the disciples out in two, Latter-Day Saint missionaries are dispersed in pairs, and Joshua and Caleb stood together to admonish the angry Israelites who had already verbally attacked Moses and Aaron (Numbers 14:1–10).

Alex Gonzalez and Brannon Walls were just third graders when they decided to use the Power of Two to become Protectors for a fellow student. He wasn't their friend, but they felt sorry for him. But they didn't just stop with sorrow. The felt indignant due to how a group of boys enjoyed bullying him in their Christian school. They did it when authority wasn't looking, often at lunchtime. The group of bullying boys attacked him for his speech impediment and for being socially awkward at times.

Alex and Brannon, unlike the majority of their peers who also went to church, broke from the herd and created tangible acts of love and righteousness by standing up for the boy. They told the bullies to "Leave him alone," words straight out of our curriculum. They invited him to sit with them at lunch. They walked him to class and helped him with his schoolbooks. They were more than kind. They were protective. That boy, who was clinically depressed, whose grades were plummeting, and who was about to leave school, got his life back. He gained confidence and dignity. He graduated as a student ready for college.

Alex, who became the starting varsity quarterback, and Brannon, one of the highest scorers on the basketball team, have graduated from high school now. But I had a chance to catch up with them before they did. They told me that standing up for a target of serial bullying felt great because they helped another person. But it also gave them courage unlike any other experience. This courage gave them additional courage to take other life-affirming risks. Alex said it helped give him courage to try out for positions in sports, like quarterback, that he probably wouldn't have.

Alex and Brannon grew up in church, doing all the usual youth group activities, including mission trips. Now please don't gloss over what I'm about to write or, rather, what Alex is about to reveal. Because it's transformational for you, your child, and our nation: "One of the things it did was renew my energy for my walk with Christ. I saw the pain that was in his face before, and I saw how Christ used us, and the joy on his face afterward. *It was honestly the only time I've experienced something like that.*"

Justice ministry was the greatest spiritual experience of his life.

Alex and Brannon are made of better stuff because they took justice and mercy seriously, strengthening their spiritual DNA. They show us what our goal as individuals and parents should be when forging a character that includes tenderness and toughness, kindness and courage.

Imagine if Alex and Brannon went to school with Alex Moore. Imagine if in Alex's school there were Christian students who sang songs of exaltation at church on Sunday, and stood up for the vulnerable on Monday. Imagine if their response to "What would Jesus do?" included "stand up for those who are abused, slandered, vilified, and scorned for no good reason." Would their love, mercy, and courage have given Alex the ballast she needed to navigate her storm?

It is possible, if not probable, that if two classmates stood up for Alex Moore, she would be alive today. And I'm confident that if those two classmates were Christians, they would have earned the respect and esteem of their peers, who would notice that there is something very different about Christians. They do more than talk—the way they hear others just talk. They act. Because they really do love others the way God wants them to. In a world full of hot air, posing, dissimulation, lies, and outright wickedness and evil, they would be forced to conclude that those Christians were different.

But I also know another truth: only about 4–8 percent of students have the stellar character to do so. This breaks God's heart, and it should grieve us as well.

The Courage Component

When the *700 Club* completed its feature story on The Protectors at Silverdale Baptist Academy, I finally had a chance to speak with Melody one-on-one. As Diane Alosi wrote, she was a small young lady. If she were fifty pounds soaking wet, I'd be surprised. She spoke with a high voice as well. Yet it was her eyes that I remember most. They held so much conviction, courage, and strength during and after the interview. She beat me to the handshake, extending her hand first. She said, "Mr. Coughlin, it's an honor to meet you." I teared up, and then said, "Oh Melody, it's an honor to meet you. I want you to run for president someday because this world needs more people like you."

Bullying represents the worst in human nature, but combatting it, the best. Melody was one of the first Protectors we had the pleasure to help inspire toward acts of tangible righteousness. That's because we know that awareness and kindness alone have never changed the world for the better. They need a third component to tether them, complete them, and activate them. That component is courage.

Courage, the foundational virtue that bolsters all other virtues, is needed in other parts of the theater of bullying as well. It's needed to acknowledge when we have wronged another, and then take that mighty step to make amends through an apology. A ninth grade teacher in Livermore, California, writes:

> After your presentation, I heard a student say, "We don't have bullying in our school." I said, "Yes, we do. I have seen it for years, and it's wrong." Later that day, in front of the entire class, a student who had been bullying another student for a long time apologized. It was one of those moments that I will remember for a very long time.

And this letter is from a fourth grade teacher in Lyons, Georgia:

> After your anti-bullying presentation, our class discussed times when we might have been bullies and when we've been bullied. One of my students apologized for writing a mean note to someone in the class just last week. She said that your bullying assembly made her realize what a horrible feeling that must have been to have received the note. The two girls went home all smiles today.

During the 2017–18 school year alone, we helped more than one thousand students find the courage they needed to publicly apologize for bullying and related behaviors during our live presentations. Too often, we underestimate what our children are willing and able to do.

Our children are far more heroic than we give them credit for. We need to raise our expectations. We have settled for low-grade goodness as a culture, as parents, and as guardians. And we've settled for low-grade goodness in church as well. We have settled for saying please and thank you, which are great, but they're not enough. We've settled for kindness—and the world needs more kindness—but kindness is fickle and unreliable when untethered from courage. We've settled for nice kids but not necessarily good kids, the kind who stand up for others. Right now, we believe that one of the most meaningful expressions of Christian faith in school is to point to Heaven after scoring a touchdown, a clutch three-point shot, a goal, or a home run. This is how we currently give glory to God.

There is a more excellent way.

Let's start putting our hand down so we can lift others up. Let's lift up that kid Alex and Brannon helped, the one who has become the object of other's ridicule, dislike, and scorn. That kid even "good kids" decide to pick on for entertainment and increased social status. Being a Protector is challenging. Yet it's where our character is forged and our esteem earned.

Because right now, this hour, the spirit of a child is going out in our country—such as this boy, who needs a Protector. His mother writes:

Dear Protectors,

My sixth grade son has hemophilia. In fourth grade, he was bullied so badly by a child the school let in (after being kicked out of public schools) that he actually wrote a letter to his teacher stating he wished he were dead. He isolated himself and refused to eat. Was mad all the time and wouldn't talk. This year he is being bullied verbally, emotionally, and now physically by the majority of students in his class. He has no self-esteem and doesn't fight back. I worry constantly that he is going to kill himself. He sobbed to me for hours tonight and I still have not been able to get him to eat.

I refuse to go through the whole process over again of "Let's try and save the bully and worry about him." This was the answer I received multiple times when I asked how exactly are you helping my son. In the process of "saving" or attempting to save the bully, they lost my son. I need him back. He is an amazing kid. I purposefully put him in a Christian private school so that the attention would be more focused on school, rather than sports, which he cannot do because of his bleeding disorder.

Please, please lecture these students and make them understand not only the damage bullying causes, but also just how anti-Christian this is. I need someone to take this seriously.

It is killing me watching my son be so totally miserable.

There is a way that's superior to lectures. It's when a child of courage and conviction stands up for such a kid, changing personal histories within the larger arc of history. May this happen in our lifetime.

After a presentation to public school elementary and middle-school students in California, a long line of students formed to speak with me, the longest I've ever seen. This school was ravaged by bullying. I could see it on the beleaguered faces of teachers who were exhausted and hopeless. I was grateful that my children did not go to such a school.

The line was so long that the school had to change the schedule for the rest of the school day in order for me to speak with each student. I'll never forget one of them. She wore a long-sleeve, baby blue blouse and had long, straight, raven-black hair parted down the middle. She wore thick glasses and was a little overweight. She was adorable.

Most students can ask their question or tell their story to me out loud. But not her. She stood before me crying. Her shoulders heaved. She could hardly speak. So I kneeled down and said, "Sweetie, it's okay. Just whisper it in my ear."

She said four words that changed my life, and I hope they change yours, too.

"Does bullying include sex?"

She was just ten years old.

I see her in almost every school I go to. The faces just change.

That innocent little angel with such a sweet spirit and tender voice does not just need a shoulder to cry on. Not ultimately anyway. What she really needs, before compassion or kindness, is a hope that tomorrow can be a better day. And that hope rides in on the courageous shoulders of others—protective shoulders large enough and loving enough to create justice for her, and millions just like her.

May our Lord help us find such courage.

Notes

[1] Timothy Keller, "Forgiving and Forgiven," February 3, 1991, from *Gospel in Life*, produced by Timothy Keller, 42:40, https://www.youtube.com/watch?v=pMJiB9fuiEA.

[2] C. S. Lewis, *Surprised by Joy: The Shape of My Early Life* (New York: Harcourt, Brace 1955), 28.

[3] For a historical look at the Asch experiment, see Knud Larsen, "The Asch Conformity Experiment: Replication and Transhistorical Comparisons," *Journal of Social Behavior and Personality* 5, no. 4 (1990): 163–68.

"You Too, Paul?"

When I was in fifth grade, I had a wise, smart, and kind classmate named Tammy. She was an old soul who was more loving than the rest of us there at Garden Grove Elementary School in Reseda, California. I remember how when she talked with people, she really listened, as if they were as important or more important than she was. She was a rare eleven-year-old.

She was rare in another way. Tammy had brain cancer. Doctors removed it through the front of her face. They left a zigzaggy scar that started in the middle of her forehead and went south to nearly the tip of her disfigured nose.

At that time, there was a popular television show for children called *Shazam*, a superhero whose mission, ironically, was to fight injustice for all people. He wore a red suit with a bold, gold-colored lightening bolt on his chest.

A group of my classmates would run up to Tammy while she was alone, point at her, and yell, "Shazam!" Then they would run away laughing and congratulating one another. They're bullying angered me. So I defended her, telling them "Stop!" and "Leave her alone!"

But then something came over me. It was a clear, clean, and cold morning in Southern California. Before school began, I walked up to Tammy where she was seated on a bench, pointed, and called her "Shazam!"

My classmates made it look so fun. They were giddy with pleasure, and when they bullied Tammy together, it galvanized their friendship. It made them more popular.

Looking back, I suppose that I wanted what they had, the dark pleasure that comes from controlling and dominating others. I got it, though it hardly lasted because Tammy turned her long, skinny face, looked at me with tears in her hazel-blue eyes, and said, "You too, Paul?"

I ran away, laughing, but my laugh was a cowardly lie. I deliberately harmed another human being—a girl with beautiful eyes and a large soul whom I normally defended, whose only sin was that she had a cancer she didn't want but courageously bore.

I burned with shame, as all bullies should. I felt sick soon afterward, and I never did it again.

I had been helping tens of thousands combat bullying for nearly a decade before I remembered how I had intentionally harmed an innocent little girl with so much more character than me. Tammy, I have tried to find you so I can apologize, to let you know that the problem of my bullying began and ended with me, the coward, not you nor your distinctive scar. I hope this confession will find you, and it will find you doing well, because if anyone deserves a life of love and laughter, it's you.

It's a complicated theater, bullying, with its many entrances and exits, and with children playing multiple roles, and where few ever admit they play the role of Judas the villain, the way I did to Tammy.

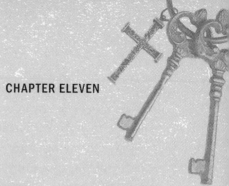

CHAPTER ELEVEN

The Coming Shalom

In a way, the world is a great liar. It shows you it worships and admires money, but at the end of the day it doesn't. It says it adores fame and celebrity, but it doesn't, not really. The world admires, and wants to hold on to, and not lose, goodness. It admires virtue. —Peggy Noonan

IF I WERE GIVEN A MAGIC WAND AND ALLOWED ONE WISH TO BESTOW UPON THE WORLD TO FIGHT BULLYING, I would not wish that teachers would do a better job of spotting it and solving it. Of course, some teachers can do a better job, and some are even derelict in their responsibilities, but I wouldn't waste my wish there. I would wish for something far more powerful: that parents and related guardians would make standing up to bullying a family value the way they currently value working hard, doing homework, and tidying rooms.

As explained earlier, bullying is a cultural problem, not a school problem. So the battleground is not the playground, but the dinner table. Researchers surveyed 1,440 fourth and fifth grade students "about how their classmates behaved in bullying situations and also did home interviews to see how parents told kids to respond to hypothetical incidents."[1] Children who said they might confront bullies and comfort targets were more likely to have parents who told them to. But what they discovered next helps us see once again that there is little neutrality in the theater of bullying. They discovered that children whose parents told them to stay out of it were less likely to help targets and *more likely to become perpetrators*. They were more likely to join the bully. Researchers speculate that children perceived that their parents' advice indicated a lack of empathy for targets, thereby justifying the bullying behavior as not being very bad.

In the movie *American Sniper*, there is a dinner conversation that needs to be replicated across our nation if we are serious about battling bullying. Chris Kyle's father tells his two sons that there are three kinds of people in this world: sheep, wolves, and sheepdogs. "I expect you to be sheepdogs," he says. Kyle's father expected him and his brother to stand up for those who cannot or will not stand up for themselves.

Those who battle international human trafficking know that in order to change the tide on this specific form of evil, they must change police departments in many parts of the world. Because in many cases, this is where the problem starts. They know that there is a small group of officers who will do the right thing, regardless of whether or not it brings them harm. And there is a small group of police officers that will do whatever it takes to get ahead—including helping sell a twelve-year-old girl into sex slavery. The majority of officers are in the middle. They could go either way. The direction they go is in the direction of power. Do the good guys have it, or the bad guys?

In order to change a police department, and in order to change individual schools across America, we need to grow the good guys.

And that number doesn't have to be all that big. We only need about 20 percent or so of students to stand up to bullying—then the herd in the middle will join them, effectively ending bullying. But we adults must make this a family value. We must make standing up to bullying, being true peacemakers who are called children of God, an essential part of our spiritual journey.

We must explain to our children how "no" is one of the most spiritual words they will ever say. We must be more like Blake and Kippi Buchanan, parents to an incredible young man, Jett.

I met this senior while speaking at Trinity Christian School in Lubbock, Texas. He was the first person I spoke with at the school. He was in the main office, and I was fresh out of my rental car when I saw him standing in front of me with a white T-shirt and blue jeans. I overheard him talking about bullying, and the way he talked made me think that he did more than dislike bullying. He acted against it.

"You talk like a Protector," I said.

"I sure am," he said.

I shook his hand and immediately liked him. I told him that most people who protect others are made, not born.

"Is protecting others something your parents taught you?" I asked.

"Yes, sir," he said in a confident and friendly tone.

"Jett, I want to interview your parents, because they're doing it right," I said.

During our interview later that day, Blake said that he and his wife, Kippi, were intentional about rearing men (not boys), and part of being a man is helping and protecting others. "During prayer time, I would always say, 'Lord, help us to always protect the weak and defend the innocent." Kippi said she writes in the cards she gives them, "The Lord will give you eyes to see and hear the needs of others."

Faith, said Blake, is emulating what Jesus did for us. "If you serve others, protect others—that is what faith looks like."

Jett told me that when he looks at the life of Jesus, he doesn't see Jesus "hanging out with the Pharisees and the big powerful people. He's hanging out with the prostitutes and tax collectors." Jett realized, as we all must, "If I'm always hanging out with the popular group, then I need to go out and reach out and bring other people in with me. I need to hang out with others who don't fit in, who don't have a good thing. You raise them up; it's leadership. You don't really know how good this feels until you actually do it."

Jett told me about an eighth grader with Down syndrome who always comes up to him and gives him high fives and fist bumps. "I saw him in the lunchroom and saw him always eating by himself, secluded. So I sat with him and before you know it, other people came over and sat with me. And I said, 'No, you're sitting with us.' Before you know it they're engaging with him as well."

Kippi said that in order for kids to stand up to bullying at school, it has to begin at home with siblings. "It starts in the home, early, in how you allow your kids to treat each other. I have never allowed being mean to other people. It's never justified, and it hurts me when people hurt," she said, holding her right hand to her throat and heart. "I hope I instilled this in my boys, because I love people and God loves everyone."

Jett said that we are to love God and people, "Not just certain people."

Blake and Kippi are proud of their son. Blake ended the interview by kissing his son on the head. And they should be proud. Jett is a co-student body leader. He's an example of how leadership isn't telling other people what to do, but showing them how, and including others as well. Jett put some of his social capital on the line when he identified with the eighth grader with Down syndrome. It was a sacrifice, or at least a potential sacrifice, he was willing to make in order to follow Jesus.

Blake and Kippi's prayers with their three sons include more than just the three Ss that occupy most of our prayers for our children: safety, security, and success. Their prayers also include the well-being of others, and the role their sons play in the well-being of others. Theirs is a religion of "we," not just "us," and the results are noticeable.

Courageous love is contagious. What's needed for others to catch it and to start a revival of love is for just one person to break some kind of social barrier, such as identifying with a marginalized child the way Jett did, or break free from some kind of psychological barrier, which in most cases is some form of fear that includes the sin of cowardice. Then others will follow and do the same thing. We see this all across the country during our live presentations where after the first person apologizes for bullying, others will do it as well. Courage is almost as contagious as fear. And we people of faith have a great example. Jesus was such a barrier breaker. He showed us how to do it, and he expects us to do it as well. This is our hope, and it's also our challenge as parents and related caregivers.

Harvard's Making Caring Common project contributes to the literature of moral development and how parents and caregivers can raise caring, ethical children. One way they do this, says codirector Richard Weissbourd, is to access what we currently emphasize regarding parenting. And what we're currently doing is pretty depressing. They asked numerous students what was most important to their parents. They're answers were almost exclusively their self-esteem, their happiness, and their achievements. There was hardly a mention about how they treated others.[2]

To rear children who are caring, kind, and courageous and who care about justice for others, we adults have to value these attributes more than we currently do. And the solution, he says, is simple. Say that the most important thing to me as a parent isn't that you're happy, "but that you are kind and happy." That you are successful, and also caring and compassionate. That you have strong self-esteem, and you are also courageous enough to help raise the esteem of others.

To cultivate caring hearts and kindness in your children, Weissbourd says to not let your child write off other children whom they find annoying. Ask them to reach out to friendless kids on the playground. Make sure they are respectful to your friends. Require them to write thank-you notes. "These things might not be so fun to them, or make them happy in the moment, but are things that build their capacity for respect, care and kindness."[3]

Expand Their Circle of Concern

Bullies, even serial bullies, care about people, so they are capable of related behaviors like kindness and compassion. The problem is their circle of concern is too small. The same can be true for witnesses as well as targets. "Most kids have empathy. The question is, who do they have empathy for?" asks Weissbourd. They may have empathy for members of their family and pets, but not for the bus driver or waitress. Weissbourd says that to rear children of character, we must help put others on our children's moral radar, helping them humanize those outside their constricted circle of concern.

And now for the painful part, at least for me. Weissbourd asks: Are we modeling these behaviors to our children? Are we extending kindness, empathy, courage, and a concern for justice toward others? Are we contributing to our communities? Or are we only focused on our children and not other kids on the playing field? "Kids will pick up our qualities and want to be like us if they respect us," he concludes.

I play Weissbourd's video during my parent presentations when I have time because it's that important. It also helps me make up for my own sins, I hope. I am also guilty of what Weissbourd points out. As the father of three children, I have also focused too much upon my own children without much thought for other children. I wanted my children to be courageous and successful, and they are; yet at the same time, I should have emphasized the value of others more than I did.

Battling bullying begins, but doesn't end, with parents, guardians, and related caregivers. A 2017 study of 1,440 fourth and fifth graders published in the *Journal of Clinical Child and Adolescent Psychology* revealed that a child is more likely to become a protector if their parents told them to help targets. The same survey revealed that children who were told to not help a target were more likely to support the bully or become bullies themselves, proving once again that there is little if any neutrality in the theater of bullying. [4]

With the same magic wand mentioned at the beginning of this chapter, I would make further changes to parenting, including:

- Banish coercive parenting styles, because they are linked to the creation of bullies.
- Banish unearned praise and adulation for children, because this also can lead to an arrogant and entitled orientation toward others.
- Correct the belief among many Christian parents that their child is required to accept abusive behavior from other children through a tortured interpretation of "turn the other cheek" and related Scriptures.
- Banish selfish parenting, because such children are far less likely to be Protectors.

- Banish over-parenting, because it's linked to the creation of narcissistic children who may bully, and also timid children who are ideal targets for bullying.
- Put spiritual courage on our spiritual radar where it can do more than diminish bullying, but also create faith, courage, and character for life.

More Authoritative Communities

It takes a community to battle bullying—that circle of concern that Weissbourd extols, both inside and outside our schools. Specifically, it takes what a band of diverse and trail-blazing researchers called "Authoritative Communities."

This study, created by the Commission on Children at Risk in 2003, gave to those who really care about children, "The new scientific age for authoritative communities."[5] Comprised of thirty-three children's doctors, research scientist, and mental health and youth service professionals, the commission's findings were dire then and are prophetic now. It warned our nation and the world about a coming wave of adolescent depression, anxiety, attention deficit, conduct disorders, and thoughts of suicide. And our current use of medications and psychotherapies, though necessary, aren't enough to stem this dangerous tide. "More and more," it warns, "what is harming and killing our children today is mental illness, emotional distress, and behavioral problems."

This is especially troubling in the theater of bullying since a bullied child is far more likely to be a depressed child, and an anxious child is more likely to be culled from the group and bullied, creating a vicious cycle of abuse and self-abuse.

What's needed is to improve the environmental conditions that kids live in, and this is accomplished through "two kinds of connectedness—close connections to other people, and deep connections to moral and spiritual meaning." Essentially, "science is increasingly demonstrating the human person is hardwired to connect . . . hardwired for meaning, born with a built-in capacity and drive to search for purpose and reflect on life's ultimate ends. . . . Ignoring the moral needs of children can be a form of child neglect."

Meeting this deep need for connectedness, the experts conclude, isn't found in yet another group of experts. It's found through us, people who may not have letters behind our names but who have wise and sacred words on our hearts and whose common bond is a commitment to love—"groups of people who are committed to one another over time and who model and pass on at least part of what it means to be a good person and live a good life."[6] We don't have to be smart, brilliant, or gifted. We just need to show up and be there for children.

There is a finer point in this remarkable study that is especially important within the theater of bullying. It has to do with how adolescents are prone to idealize themselves and others, even if neither deserves it. To compensate for such misjudgment, a civil society must "expose young people to morally admirable persons," which sounds easier than it is, because the adolescent mind is prone to mistake celebrity for admirability. It's prone to put a bully like Gordon Ramsey in the same category as a hero returning from war, for example. Youth need wise guidance to discern the difference.

They, write the authors of *Hardwired to Connect*, also need help getting over themselves in order to obtain a mature moral identity through "a profound redirection of the idealizing tendency," away from themselves and upon "some worthy version of otherness." Specifically, "we can say that adulthood has been achieved when narcissism is transmuted, and thereby detoxified. . . . The true adult venerates ideal versions of his community, his vocation and his family."[7]

Serial bullies don't transmute and detoxify naturally or well on their own. We as a people of goodwill must help them through this transformation. Teachers alone can't do it, even the more heroic ones. And a growing number of parents need help with basic parenting. Parenting expert Leonard Sax writes:

> We Americans have gone far astray in the past three decades with regard to understanding what kids need to become fulfilled and independent adults. We have undermined the authority of teachers and parents. We have allowed kids to be guided by same-age peers rather than insisting on the primacy of guidance from adults. As a result, American kids now grow up to be less imaginative, less adaptive, and less creative than they could be.[8]

Not only must we move them to the idealization of morally strong people; we need to be this kind of person as well. We can all be elders in the lives of children. We can be oracles, part of what *Hardwired* calls "extra-familial adult relationships for young people." These "protective" relationships with adults of goodwill guard children from themselves, and the culture they create and cherish, which in many ways can be an extension of their own narcissism. "This sense of connectedness to adults is salient as a protective factor against an array of health-jeopardizing behaviors of adolescents and has protective effects for both girls and boys across various ethnic, racial and social class groups."[9]

This surprisingly faith-friendly study made an initial splash but has lost its appeal more than a decade later. We must insert this study and its solutions back into the public square if we are serious about battling bullying and protecting our children. It reminds us of how religiosity and spirituality are "positively associated with . . . lower levels of stress hormones (cortisol), more optimism, and commitment to helping others." About 96 percent of American teenagers say they believe in God, and this belief can also lead to less hypertension and depression, "a lower risk of suicide, less criminal activity, and less use and abuse of drugs and alcohol." People who are religiously active also benefit from larger social networks and more social contact and support.[10]

Personal devotion to the Divine among adolescents, it reports, "is associated with more effectively resolving feelings of loneliness, greater regard for the self and for others, and a strong sense that life has meaning and purpose." But here is where it gets really interesting. These protective effects of personal devotion with the Divine are "twice as great for adolescents as they are for adults."

Denying or ignoring the spiritual needs of adolescents "may end up creating a void in their lives that either devolves into depression or is filled by other forms of questing and challenge, such as drinking, unbridled consumerism, petty crime, sexual precocity, or flirtations with violence." Drinking, petty crime, and flirtations with violence are common behaviors associated with adolescent bullying as well. The report concludes with strong language: "Pretending that children's religious and spiritual needs do not exist, or arguing that it is too hard to address them in ways that respect individual conscience and pluralism, is for an authoritative community a form of denial and even self-defeat."[11]

Battling bullying is the church's most unrecognized mission field, a cause that will draw the attention, affection, and respect of communities across the country. That's because the human heart and mind are created to admire *shalom*, and to mourn its loss. Bullying is the leading form of child abuse in the nation and throughout the world. It's the leading concern and worry of both parents and students. It's a massive cultural problem and is the most under-recognized Civil Rights issue of our time that denies equal access to an education, among other problems both legally and personally. Adolescent bullying represents some of the worst miscarriages of justice in our country and our world. It needs the church to stand against it.

Shrewdness of Serpents for Targets

As described previously, many so-called Christian solutions to bullying are big on zeal but not on knowledge or wisdom when it comes to the real theater of bullying. One reason why is because we've failed to really learn from Jesus, who told us to exercise the shrewdness of serpents as we go into perilous situations, such as bullying (Matt. 10:16).

Instead of telling our children to acquiesce by admonishing them to turn the other cheek, we must arm them with sharp and perceptive powers of judgment instead. One reason why this is so important is because the rules within almost every institution are stretched by bullies to favor bullies. Targets are far more prone to follow the rules, even when those rules work against them. And these rules are not handed down from Mount Sinai and chiseled in stone since time began. They aren't written in our Constitution.

Here's one example: Many schools have a policy that doesn't allow a target of physical bullying to use physical force to defend himself. But policy isn't law, and policy can violate the law. Legislation has been proposed in at least one state that challenges this policy against common-sense self-defense. It's possible that such a policy violates the rights of adolescents in America. But it's still policy. It's still a rule; but it doesn't make it right, fair, or "Christian."

We must shrewdly realign our response to the crooked theater of bullying if we're serious about rescuing targets. And when in doubt, our rules, policies, and laws should always favor the target.

True children of light are more subversive and pugnacious than we realize at first glance. Let's think shrewdly and outside the box because our children are too important not to. Theologian Reinhold Niebuhr said it more eloquently:

> The children of light must be armed with the wisdom of the children of darkness but remain free from their malice. They must know the power of self-interest in human society without giving it moral justification. They must have this wisdom in order that they may beguile, deflect, harness and restrain self-interest, individual and collective, for the sake of the community.[12]

Let me give you an example from my own life. My eldest son, Elliot, at one time loved to bully his younger brother, Garrett. Elliot is built like a German farmhand. He's big and strong, even when he's not lifting weights. Garrett is more like me; built like his Irish grandfather (the Irish aren't exactly big people—we're more like large elves). So when Elliot bullied his brother, Garrett would punch him as hard as he could. But Elliot, being two years older and much more stocky, would just laugh. Again and again. Then Garrett would get in trouble for screaming. I'm ashamed to say that I did not catch on to this dynamic sooner, especially since I experienced similar treatment as a kid. But eventually, I caught on, and sat them down and leveled the unfair balance of power.

I said, "Elliot, I know you're bullying your brother, and I know that you think it's funny when it's not. We've talked about it many times and for some reason you've chosen to continue. So Garrett, you now have permission to bite your brother as hard as you can. The only place you can't bite him is on the face. A great place to bite him is the back of his upper arm because it really hurts. And if I were you, I would sneak up on him and surprise him, the way he surprises you with bullying."

Suddenly a halo grew over Elliot's sweaty head. His bullying drastically reduced overnight. And no, I did not teach my son that "violence is the answer." He did not become a violent person, beating up other kids for the fun of it. I taught my son to defend his own value, dignity, and worth, all three given to him by God.

Today, they are best friends and fiercely look out for each other's best interests. They were roommates in college, living in an apartment the size of a glorified closet with running water. They have a brotherly love I always wanted and did not get. But I helped make this happen for my sons, and it's among my greatest achievements.

I know of another father who was also at the end of his rope because of bullying. He told the younger target to take off his shirt. He sprayed his back down with water, smeared salt on it, and told the older bully to lick the salt off.

The bully licked his brother's back and cried.

His brother cried.

The serial bullying ended.

I know this sounds extreme to many people, especially those who have the gift of being easily offended. Matters of the heart and soul may appear extreme when you aren't being harmed. But I would bet that to those who have been on the receiving end of bullying, these examples of liberation do not appear extreme. In fact, those who have been bullied wish someone had orchestrated such freedom for them.

The No Bullying TV Pledge

The coarsening of our society comes at us from many directions: violent lyrics, video games, social media, and television, especially reality television. Since reality television comes the closest to how children perceive reality, we as a culture should concentrate our limited time and energy upon this cultural influencer that too often glamorizes bullying, which expert Barbara Coloroso reminds us is "arrogance in action." This arrogance comes at us every day through millions of pixels. We have two ways of approaching this problem. One is to pledge not to watch it in our homes, which will hit these programs where it really hurts, financially (the exact same dynamic that has removed bullying pastors from the pulpit). And such a boycott would show our disapproval of bullying to our children as well.

Our other option is to watch reality television with our children and point out examples of bullying, which I have done myself. This approach has an amazing way of ruining reality television for your kids—ruining it in a good way. Point out that what's being done to the person who is on the receiving end isn't funny or justified. Say things like, "No one should be treated that way." Point out how yelling and screaming at another person, a staple in the *Real Housewives* syndication, is no way to solve problems, but is a great way to abuse another human being.

Protectors Freedom Council

Social justice is a growing desire and problem in our country, yet few schools give students the opportunity to work on behalf of justice. This is one reason why we created the Protectors Freedom Council (PFC). It's a grassroots, student-led club (with a trusted advisor) that keeps freedom-from-bullying efforts alive on school campuses.

Schools have been creative in how they implement this program. One private Christian school has every third-grade student become a Protector for two weeks. A letter is sent to the parents explaining what the school is doing and why. Each student meets with a school counselor before the student is given permission to look for and report incidents of bullying and related behavior. Then each student meets with the school counselor after the two weeks is over in order to debrief and talk about their experience.

Another private Christian school unfolds the PFC in sixth grade, and students can't wait to join. We know this because during their graduation ceremony going into sixth grade, numerous students mention how they are looking forward to learning how to better protect themselves and others from bullying.

The Irving Independent School District in Texas has an estimated thirty-five thousand students using The Protectors program. When one of its high schools implemented the PFC, they witnessed immediate results. The president of the PFC, senior Walter Veliz, was walking down the hall when a ninth grader stopped him and asked him for help. He explained that there was no way he was going to tell a teacher about how he was being bullied. And he didn't want to tell his parents either. But in the unwritten code of adolescent life, it was okay to talk to an older student, especially a popular one who has taken a public stand against bullying. Veliz helped the student and the bullying ended almost overnight.

Other efforts proven to diminish bullying include the following:

Anti-Bullying Pledges

They may appear corny, but they work. Create a competition to see which class or which grade can come up with the most comprehensive and inspiring pledge. Some schools put this pledge in the main entry, and some also put the pledge in bullying hot spots, like certain bathrooms and certain parts of locker rooms. One Christian school we know puts anti-bullying Scriptures in bathrooms where bullying has been a problem.

Anonymous Reporting

Studies show that students are more likely to report bullying if they don't appear on the bully's radar, and anonymous reporting is a great way to make this happen. STOP!T, created by Todd Schrobel, a passionate anti-bullying crusader, has been named by CNN as one of the top five apps changing the world for good. Not only does STOP!T reduce bullying; in some cases, it has been reduced by up to 50 percent. It can also help schools reduce the wasted time looking into false reports of bullying—in some cases, up to 75 percent. In September 2017, Texas enacted one of the most substantive anti-cyberbullying laws in the United States that requires school districts to implement anonymous reporting because it's so effective. More states should follow its leadership.

Play Gentle Music during Recess

A first-of-its-kind study from Israel found that gentle melodies may help deter bullying. The three-week experiment featured fifty-six students at a local elementary school in Northern Israel. All were either eleven or twelve years old. For the first week, the researchers quietly observed the kids during their twenty-minute mid-day recess. For three days of the second week, relaxing music was played on speakers throughout the recess, reducing bullying. For the third week, the music was turned off, and recess proceeded as before. Bullying increased when the music was turned off, but not at previous levels, suggesting that the music's calming influence continued after it was turned off.[13]

Encourage Cyber-Supporting

At the end of my presentation while speaking to the high schoolers at Prestonwood Christian Academy in Plano, Texas, I challenged the students to cyber-support one another by only saying positive comments about their classmates on social media. Fifty-three minutes later, an administrator walked up to me with a huge smile on his face and said, "You're going to love this." A student created such a Twitter account. It had 159 followers within 53 minutes. Let that sink in for a moment. That was nearly half of the student body within less than an hour. Our children want to help, love, and support one another. We've got to give them the inspiration. expectation, creativity, and tools to do it.

Sports Programs Need to Change

It is important to make anti-bullying training mandatory for coaches. During one episode of *The Simpsons*, Homer holds up a can of Duff beer and says, "Beer, the source, and solution, to all of life's problems." This is how I feel about sports programs, especially high school sports, and bullying. With the wrong adult leadership, just one team can destroy a school through bullying and related behavior such as hazing.

As a certified high school coach, I was required each year to take additional online training to keep my certification. Yet none of my online classes even addressed the growing problem of bullying. This is a dangerous oversight that must be corrected across the nation. And I would be negligent if I did not call out football. Of all the complaints we receive at The Protectors involving a sports program, more than 90 percent involve football players *and coaches*. Just because someone complains doesn't mean their complaint is factual. But this percentage is so overwhelming that a school is foolish to ignore it. There is something wrong with football culture in America, and smart schools are addressing it head on. (I helped get a bullying and abusive football coach fired with very little effort. He didn't even try to hide his bullying, and seemed stunned that anyone would disagree with his harassing behavior. Like most bullies, he was proud of his arrogance and never admitted to any wrongdoing.)

But get amazing high school football coaches like Joe Erhmann—creator of the remarkable *Inside Out Coaching* model, which creates better athletes and better citizens—and a sports program can lead a school out of a bullying mentality. Erhmann is the subject of the excellent book *Season of Life: A Football Star, a Boy, a Journey to Manhood.* In this book, you discover that if a young man played for Joe's team, he is expected to sit next to fellow students who are eating alone at lunchtime. Erhmann helped create great football players and great people, and he's far from alone.

Matt Labrum made national news in 2013 when he suspended nearly his entire football team at Union High School in Roosevelt, Utah, for bad behavior that included bullying. Players had to earn their privilege to play again, and most did, just before the big homecoming game. "Our staff of twelve coaches were all on board," he told me. "We sat down for three hours after practice to talk about this decision. We want to win games; but more importantly, we want to help form good men. It wasn't like we had a group of really bad kids. But we wanted to help make them better."

Matt said he would do it again, though he wasn't prepared for the media onslaught that came with his coaching staff's decision. "I look back on my life when I was playing football and I looked up to my coaches. We wanted to be the same example to our players. For some, our example may be the only positive thing they experienced that day. They are more than athletes to us. We want to help them do positive things in their lives. I want our community and our kids protected. I feel like we as a people need to raise the bar and stop being the silent majority. We need to work against what's wrong in the world."

Erhmann, Labrum, and many other football coaches want to help forge the kind of character shown by Carson Jones and Tucker Workman, starting varsity players at Queens Creek High School in Arizona. In 2012, they helped special needs student Chy Johnson, who functioned at a third-grade level due to a genetic birth defect. Since physically and mentally challenged children are the most bullied, true to script, students threw trash at her and called her "stupid," among other derogatory names.

"She'd come home every night at the start of the school year crying and upset," says her mom, Liz Johnson. "That permanent smile she had, that gleam in her eye, that was all gone."[14]

Johnson says that going to school officials didn't help. So she contacted Jones who once escorted Chy to the Special Olympics. "Just keep your ear to the ground," Liz wrote to Carson on his Facebook page. "Maybe get me some names?"

But Jones went the extra mile. He invited Chy to sit with him and his friends at the cool kid's lunch table. "I just thought that if they saw her with us every day, maybe they'd start treating her better," Carson says.

Starting running back Tucker Workman made sure someone walked with Chy between classes. Cornerback Colton Moore made sure she sat in the row right behind the team as well. Not only did the bullying decrease, Chy told a reporter, "They saved me." Volleyball player Shelly Larson said, "I think about how sweet these boys are to her, and I want to cry. I can't even talk about it."

I play a news story about these brave and loving young men and what they did for Chy during our presentations to high school students. A holy hush falls upon the student body, which I wished more adults could witness, because it would challenge so many belittling stereotypes about today's youth. Too many adults think that kids don't care about others. But they do. They just need the adults in their lives to spur them on. They need to see examples of *shalom*, and they will be inspired to do the same. They just need pockets of time and self-reflection, which our presentations provide.

After the clip is played, I ask, "Ladies, tell me, are those boys attractive?" Giggles ripple throughout the gymnasium or auditorium. Carson and Tucker, the two featured in the news story, are handsome young men. But, they are more than handsome. They are good. They transcend mere physical attraction because they glow in another and far more important way. They glow in meaning and virtue, the way all of us really want to.

I don't know Carson, but I'm confident that his devout faith drove him to commit such a beautiful act of righteousness. He belongs to The Church of Jesus Christ of Latter-Day Saints, which has taken on the topic of bullying in its media. I'm not a member of the LDS Church, but I was in the church's office building in Salt Lake City when they released their video message calling their youth to combat bullying. It's a beautiful message of love and kindness that I have yet to see produced by any evangelical church, which is currently missing in this important cause. It is well past time evangelicals join the battle.

Lionize Moral Courage Whenever Possible

And finally, if I could complete my tour of the magic wound, I would compel our nation and the world to celebrate acts of courage whenever possible. Right now, we're celebrating acts of physical courage each school day through the exaltation of sports. No nation defends its borders without physical courage. I have been knocked out five times, broken my leg in two places, separated my shoulder, broken my ribs, and broken my hand all playing soccer. So, I know something about physical courage. Moral courage is far more important. For reasons explained earlier, it's the missing piece on our bullying puzzle. We applaud what we appreciate and value. We need to applaud moral courage more than we are. Because more violent tragedies that tear at the heart of *shalom* are coming. More bullied boys will pick up guns and rampage upon the student body in order to level out the power scale in their school. Statistically, they won't even shoot their bullies, because that's what rage does. It's powerlessness in disguise, a vomiting of pain and suffering. So it spews.

But the fallout of bullying is usually far less dramatic. We will never hear about the majority of it, but we will see its affect. We will see it in the lives of the walking wounded among us, the ones with the fake smiles who just can't seem to get their lives together as adults. They are the ones who can't commit because they lack the ability to trust. They are the ones with actual low self-esteem who have a hard time controlling their anger. They lash out at the oddest times, losing friends and sometimes jobs. But most of all, they're the resentful ones, where their resentment is their last desperate and dangerous stab at self-respect.

Youth culture is too broken and the abuse of bullying too prevalent to expect children to transform the theater of bullying alone. We people of faith are late to the battle. But we're not too late. We still have time to be the hands and heart of God in our communities, creating tangible expressions of love, courage, and kindness, to God's glory and to the benefit of man.

Notes

[1] Lisa Rapport, "Kids More Likely to Stop Bullies When Parents Tell Them to," Health News, April 13, 2017, accessed on April 15, 2018, http://www.reuters.com/article/us-health-children-bullying-parents-idUSKBN17F20Q/.

[2] "Making Caring Common Project," Harvard Graduate School of Education, accessed on April 15, 2018, https://mcc.gse.harvard.edu.

[3] "Making Caring Common Project."

[4] Lisa Rapport, "Kids More Likely to Stop Bullies When Parents Tell Them To," *Reuters Health News,* April 13, 2017, https://www.reuters.com/article/us-health-children-bullying-parents/kids-more-likely-to-stop-bullies-when-parents-tell-them-to-idUSKBN17F20Q.

[5] Commission on Children at Risk, *Hardwired to Connect: The New Scientific Case for Authoritative Communities* (New York: Broadway Publications, 2003).

[6] Commission on Children at Risk, *Hardwired to Connect,* 9.

[7] Commission on Children at Risk, *Hardwired to Connect,* 20.

[8] Leonard Sax, *The Collapse of Parenting: How We Hurt Our Kids When We Treat Them Like Grown-Ups* (New York: Basic Books, 2016), 300.

[9] Commission on Children at Risk, *Hardwired to Connect,* 140.

[10] Commission on Children at Risk, *Hardwired to Connect,* 22.

[11] Commission on Children at Risk, *Hardwired to Connect,* 30.

[12] Reinhold Niebuhr, *The Children of Light and the Children of Darkness: a Vindication of Democracy and a Critique of Its Traditional Defenses* New York: C. Scribner and Sons, 1947), 40–41.

[13] Tom Jacobs, "Background Music Reduces Playground Bullying," April 24, 2013, *Pacific Standard,* https://psmag.com/education/background-music -reduces-playground-bullying-56156/.

[14] Rick Reilly, "Special Team," ESPN, November 1, 2012, accessed on April 15, 2018, http://www.espn.com/espn/story/_/id/8579599/chy-johnson-boys.

Recommended Reading

Brooks, David. *The Road to Character*. New York: Random House, 2015.

Cloud, Henry, and John Townsend. *Boundaries: When to Say Yes, How to Say No to Take Control of Your Life*. 2nd ed. Grand Rapids: Zondervan, 2017.

Coloroso, Barbara. *Bully, the Bullied, and the Not-So-Innocent Bystander: From Preschool to High School and Beyond: Breaking the Cycle of Violence and Creating More Deeply Caring Communities*. New York: William Morrow, 2016.

Coloroso, Barbara. *Extraordinary Evil: A Short Walk to Genocide*. New York: Nation Books, 2007.

Commission on Children at Risk, The. *Hardwired to Connect: The New Scientific Case for Authoritative Communities*. New York: Broadway Publications, 2003.

Evans, Patricia. *Verbal Abuse: Survivors Speak Out on Relationship and Recovery*. Avon, MA: Adams Media, 2003.

Keller, Timothy. *Walking with God through Pain and Suffering*. New York: Penguin Books, 2016.

King, Martin Luther, Jr. *Strength to Love*. Minneapolis: Fortress Press, 2010.

Palacio, R. J. *Wonder*. New York: Alfred A. Knopf, 2012.

Shouten, Ronald, and James Silver. *Almost a Psychopath: Do I (or Does Someone I Know) Have a Problem with Manipulation and Lack of Empathy?* Center City, MN: Hazelden Publishing, 2012.

Shroeder, David A., Louis A. Penner, John F. Dovidio, and Jane A. Piliavin. *The Psychology of Helping and Altruism: Problems and Puzzles*. New York: McGraw-Hill, 1995.

Townsend, John. *Beyond Boundaries: Learning to Trust Again in Relationships*. Grand Rapids: Zondervan, 2011.

Twenge, Jean M., and W. Keith Cambell. *The Narcissism Epidemic: Living in the Age of Entitlement*. New York: Atria Books, 2009.

Worthington, Everett L, Jr. *How Do I Forgive?* Downers Grove, IL: InterVarsity Press, 2012.

Zimbardo, Philip. *The Lucifer Effect: Understanding How Good People Turn Evil*. New York: Random House, 2007.